Ford Mustang Buyer's & Restoration Guide

Ford Mustang Buyer's & Restoration Guide

1964½–2007

PETER C. SESSLER
AND NILDA M. SESSLER

Indianapolis

All photographs © by Peter C. Sessler, except where noted. Special thanks to Jerry Heasley, Brad Bowling, and Ford Motor Company. We recognize that some words, model names and designations, for example, mentioned herein are the property of the trademark holder. We use them for identification purposes only. This is not an official publication.

International Standard Book Number: 0-7906-1326-3

Chief Executive Officer:	Alan Symons
President:	Scott Weaver
Chief Financial Officer:	Keith Siergiej
Chief Operating Officer:	Richard White
Acquisitions Editor:	Brad Schepp
Editorial Assistant:	Heidy Nathan
Editorial Assistant:	Dana Eaton
Copy Editor:	Laura Town
Pagination Editor:	Cheryl Hoffman
Cover Design:	Mike Walsh
Interior & CD Photos:	Provided by the author, Ford Motor Company, Jerry Heasley, Greg Coston, Gary Baum, and Brad Bowling

Manufactured in the USA.

Contents

Contents

Preface

The Ford Mustang has become as much a part of the American identity as apple pie, Mother, and the right to go anywhere in the United States at anytime, for any reason whatsoever (just like wild horse herds). As an icon it has also come to represent not only the freedom of youth but also the capacity to drive fast and look very, very good while doing it. The myriad of models, options, and performance levels that classic Mustangs have been available in has also strongly keyed into the American desire for individuality and self-determination. And lest we forget: many a mild-mannered Mustang owner has allowed his Boss 429 or Cobra to speak for the wild, aggressive spirit kept well-hidden inside.

Besides all of the positives that these classics have to recommend them—beauty, speed, the pleasure to own and drive—collector Mustangs have also become a very decent investment. Although non-performance Mustangs have seen their value stabilize over the years, performance Mustangs have attracted the attention of collectors with deep pockets. As a result they are fetching prices that would have been unheard-of when they were first built.

A common question asked by the uninitiated is, why does a car that was built in the millions have any collector value at all? The answer is that although performance Mustangs received tremendous hype and promotion, they were never built in great numbers. Indeed, most of the surviving classic Mustangs have become appreciating collectibles. Here it is important to make a distinction in an arena that has become increasingly confusing—the operative term is "High Performance" or "Performance" Mustangs. Although properly optioned-out Mustangs, particularly convertibles and some fastbacks, have squeaked into the collector category, the great mass of non-performance Mustangs have not made it there yet.

It would also be a mistake to assume that a non-performance Mustang costs less to buy and restore than a Boss 429, Shelby, or Cobra. It could cost as much as or more than a performance car, depending on the model, condition, and availability of parts. After-market parts abound for the most popular models, and popularity is dominated by the performance Mustangs. The value of the end product can also differ dramatically. The bottom line is that you can spend just as much restoring a 1966 six-cylinder notchback as a 1966 GT convertible. The following chapters will show why the GT convertible is a better financial investment.

Information is also provided to help you decide which type of Mustang you might be most interested in owning, and to what extent you want to become involved in upgrading, individualizing, or restoring a classic or collector model. Just be aware that Mustangs without collector status should be acquired with the idea of buying, restoring, and owning them for the enjoyment, and not as an investment that will double in value within a few years.

If you are considering acquiring a Mustang as an investment, it is important that you take the time to get an idea of what Mustangs are selling for. Publications such as *Hemmings, Old Cars Price Guide,* and Mustang club newsletters are good resources. Recently, there has been a great deal of volatility in the pricing of some Mustangs that lack the historical significance and rarity to warrant such high prices. Be discriminating, and take your time deciding which Mustang you are interested in. In this book you will learn about limited edition models that may become valuable simply because not many of them are surviving the ravages of time and neglect. They may not be as exciting as the performance Mustangs but they have the potential to serve as a stable value investment that is fun to drive and show off at car shows. Or you may find that a particular model wins your heart, and the process becomes a labor of love that provides its own rewards, with the collector status of the Mustang coming as a bonus.

The Mustang, with its long options list (which got longer as the years went on) was designed to appeal to diverse groups of buyers, but the youth factor with its need to establish individuality was always an important ingredient. Although the variety of options available for the different models is great for owners not too concerned with an exact restoration, it's a nightmare for the prospective Mustang collector. This book will help you wade through the options.

If you've already caught the Mustang bug, you can look in the publications mentioned earlier or on the Internet to see what is available, but your best bet, at least initially, is to go to some Mustang shows. Most Mustang shows are held from early spring to late fall. *Mustang Monthly* magazine publishes a good list of upcoming events, as does *Hemmings*. Going to shows is fun and educational. There's usually a good variety of cars in the typical Mustang show turnout, and nothing compares to seeing the cars and colors for yourself. Most Mustang owners are more than happy to talk (sometimes at great length!) about their cars. But you also have to be cautious because some information currently in circulation is simply wrong.

This guide treats each year of the first generation Mustangs, from 1965 through 1973, separately chapter by chapter. The exception is the 1971–72 Mustangs, which are combined in their own chapter. Second generation Mustangs, those built from 1974 through 1978, are covered in a chapter of their own. These Mustangs aren't in the same league as the first generation cars, but they do have a solid core of support. Some of the Mustangs built during those years are worthy of consideration. Third generation Mustangs, from 1979 through 1993, are also covered in a separate chapter. This chapter debunks the belief popular during the 1970s and 1980s that modern Mustangs don't compare well with the originals. The truth is that third-generation Mustangs, particularly the GTs built from 1985 to 2004, can stand on their own and offer exceptional performance and handling. Of course, the new 2005 and later Mustangs are in a class of their own, combining the looks of the late 1960s performance Mustangs with current state of the art performance and handling.

Occasionally, you may run into a Mustang that doesn't quite fit published specifications in terms of optional equipment or color. We provide the information necessary to identify Mustangs that were ordered in colors other than those initially listed. Such cars had no color code on the data plate. And it is possible to run across Mustangs equipped with options or in combinations that don't normally occur, as a result of a special order or manufacturing errors. If you find such a car and are interested in it, use this guide as a stepping stone towards researching its history and authenticity.

We have also included chapters on Mustang restoration, detailing, and maintenance. These chapters will give you a sense of what it takes to restore and keep that special Mustang running smoothly.

The Ford Mustang created great excitement when it was first introduced. There have been other Pony cars, but the Mustang was the original, and has managed to retain that special magic. Whether you buy one as an investment, a restoration project, or simply to drive and enjoy, you'll be joining a growing fraternity of very happy and enthusiastic people.

Peter C. & Nilda M. Sessler
Citrus Springs, FL
February 2006

Introduction

Choosing and Buying Your Mustang

It is imperative to become familiar with both the Mustang model and the product lines you are interested in. Stories abound about Mustangs in mint condition holed up for years in barns, carriage houses, and sheds, but it's better to be realistic. Look for a fair price on a Mustang that you can restore or upgrade to whatever level its condition permits. Keep an eye out for the availability of parts and restoration resources as well, since these can run into prohibitive amounts when too much distance separates them from your project car.

We recommend that you buy a car which is as complete as possible or as restored as possible. It's easy to underestimate the cost of a restoration because, once it is started, the tendency is to build a brand new car, replacing parts that may not need to be replaced. Also, a good, solid low-mileage original Mustang has greater collector (therefore investment) value than a restoration loaded with reproduction parts. Original cars with a minimum of reproduction replacement parts do exist, so if your heart is set on one, keep looking. They are expensive and hard to find but worth the effort.

The important thing is to take your time while shopping for your Mustang. It's hard to be objective if your heart is beating fast, your hands are sweating, and a lump in your throat makes speaking difficult! Just slow down! It's okay to be excited but you don't want to risk missing imperfections. Have the seller give you a brief history of the vehicle. Ask to see any paperwork that may be on hand, such as a bill of sale, options list, and owner's manual. Write down the VIN, since this might be a way to run a check on the history of the car yourself. Take note of where it has been stored; clean, dry conditions are a good thing. Use your senses. Look over the exterior carefully, including the body panels, windshield, windows, doors, and any trim or original ornamentation. The condition of the gaskets and paint might give an indication of how the car has weathered. Also check out the color and consistency of all interior fluids. Note any gumminess or an off-color look to the transmission and brake fluids, as you would when buying any used car. Sniff the air around and in the car for signs of mildew or decay. Listen for grunts, groans, and squeaking of doors, trunk, and hood lids, and also note any creaking of floors. Flaking metal in or under floor panels could indicate advanced deterioration.

If the car is drivable, take it for a spin and inspect it to see what works. Note anything that doesn't function or sound right. Ask the owner to drive the car while you follow behind. This is a good way to see any telltale puffs of smoke which might indicate engine problems.

The next important thing to do is to inspect it for rust. Even a Mustang that is not drivable because it lacks an engine, wheels, and an interior might be a good buy so long as it is not overcome with rust. It will simply require more effort and parts. However, Mustangs, and most cars built in the 1960s and 1970s, are prone to rust. Rear quarter panels and front fenders are the most obvious places to look, but rocker panels, trunk, floors, and doors are all susceptible to rust. If you know that the Mustang you are looking at has had substantial body work, inspect it on a lift and also look at the condition of the floors. As with all other unibody cars, a severely rusted Mustang is simply not worth restoring unless it is a one-of-a-kind or love at first sight.

Let the seller know about any imperfections or problem areas you spot. It's likely the Mustang owner has set a price he is willing to negotiate. If you can't come to a satisfactory price, don't worry. Ford made a lot of Mustangs, and it shouldn't be too difficult to locate another.

During the past twenty years, the availability of aftermarket or reproduction parts has mush-roomed—a boon for the Mustang enthusiast. The only criticism we have heard is that this has taken the challenge out of restoring a Mustang; all you have to do is call a few toll-free numbers to order what you need. Still, the quicker your restoration is finished, the sooner you can start enjoying your Mustang.

Another point to consider is *originality*. Rare, low-production Mustangs are definitely worth more when restored to their original or stock condition. Modified Mustangs, unless modified with factory or dealer-installed options, such as the Cobra kits, are not considered within the bounds of originality and this lowers their value.

As the years have passed it has become more difficult to keep surviving Mustangs strictly original. For example, radial tires improve the ride and handling of any Mustang, but they are not considered stock except in models originally equipped with them. Familiarize yourself with which modifications are readily converted back, so that you can spot a modified Mustang with good potential for re-conversion to stock condition if necessary.

Also ask the seller about any saved parts or any parts traded for the Mustang you are buying. Our advice on originality is to go ahead and buy a modified Mustang if it makes driving it more enjoyable. Do try, however, to access as many of the original parts as possible. As long as the Mustang can easily be reconverted when it comes time to part with it, modifications should not hurt its value.

Also bear in mind that a modified Mustang is unlikely to score well in a concours competition where originality is paramount. Concours judges require strict originality down to every last bolt and wire. Everything about the car has to conform to the specifications and conditions in place when the Mustang left the Ford factory. Such cars are rarely driven, and many enthusiasts feel that part of the fun of owning a Mustang is driving it, especially the hot high-performance models. Some owners and collectors solve the dilemma by acquiring a stable of Mustangs to fill these disparate needs. You have to decide what is right for you.

Lean towards choosing a Mustang that includes a large options list. This increases the odds of your finding enough original parts and equipment to restore a car you can also enjoy driving. A Boss 302, for example, wouldn't be as good a candidate as one of the GTs because it has fewer options. Think carefully before acquiring a stock 1969 Mach 1. With its lack of power steering and power brakes, it requires a type of rigorous exercise alien to younger drivers. The powerful 428CJ Mach 1 equipped with manual steering and manual drum brakes might also not be the best choice for someone interested only in Sunday cruising. More options mean greater value and better driving pleasure.

1
1965 Mustang

PRODUCTION

Early 1965 (1964½)

65A 2dr Hardtop	92,705
76A Convertible	28,833
Total	121,538

Late 1965

63A 2dr Fastback Standard	71,303
63B 2dr Fastback Luxury	5,776
65A 2dr Hardtop Standard	372,123
65B 2dr Hardtop Luxury	22,232
65C 2dr Hardtop Bench Seats	14,905
76A Convertible Standard	65,663
76B Convertible Luxury	5,338
76C Convertible Bench Seats	2,111
Total	559,451
Total Early & Late	680,989

The new Ford Mustang was greeted with enthusiasm when it finally reached Ford dealerships on April 17, 1964. It was, and remains, Ford Motor Company's most exciting and successful car built

This was the car that eventually became the Mustang. The Mustang I was an engineering and show car in 1963, meant to show the public what the new performance look for Ford could be. The Mustang I advanced the youthful performance image of the new Ford, and it should be noted that this car was the first to carry the Mustang logo, as well as the characteristic side sculpturing.

since World War II. The Mustang was introduced at the right time, but a mediocre product would not have been as successful. It was well built and boasted great styling, a long options list, and three body styles. Ford designed it to appeal to as many buyers as possible.

All Mustangs built between March 1964 and early August 1965 were coded as 1965 models, but many enthusiasts consider those built before August 1964 to be 1964½s. This identification has become so pervasive that there are clubs, books, shows, and articles devoted to it, despite the fact that Ford titled each and every one a 1965 model. To add to the confusion there are also some legitimate differences between the 1964½s (or early 1965s) and those built after August 1964. It is possible however to find late 1965 Mustangs with parts and features that supposedly were only available on the 1964½ versions. Production changes often occur during a model year, and a manufacturer will almost always use up the existing stock of a part before switching over to its successor. It's important for the novice buyer or collector to become thoroughly familiar with the features and options for the entire model year as a way of determining any claim to authenticity of a 1964½ being considered for purchase.

The Mustang was initially offered as a hardtop or a convertible. When the fastback became available, the 2+2 really added to the Mustang's magic. The Mustang continued to be available in these three body styles until the 1973 model year.

One reason the Mustang was so phenomenally successful was its pricing. A two-door hardtop had a suggested retail price of $2,320.86. For that price you got a six-cylinder engine rated at 101hp mated to a three-speed manual transmission with a floor shifter; in fact, all Mustangs have floor mounted shifters. Manual steering with a slow 27:1 ratio and manual drum brakes measuring nine inches were standard equipment. The standard tires were blackwall 6.50 x 13 in. on

The epitome of Mustangness—a red 1965 fastback Mustang GT. What more can you say?

The convertible Mustang looked great. Its clean, uncluttered lines helped it become an enduringly desirable classic.

Everything on the Mustang was optional—that's the American way. The small side pin stripe was an option.

four-lug 13-inch rims (on V-8s, 14-inch rims replaced the 13 inchers after September 1964). Obviously, such a Mustang would not be much fun to drive with such a small footprint on the road.

In the front the Mustang had an independent suspension with coil springs mounted over the upper A-arm. The rear suspension was a solid axle on leaf springs—basic but dependable.

The interior was originally available in five different all-vinyl colors, with the hardtops also getting two additional cloth-and-vinyl combinations, black or Palomino. After the summer of 1964, the cloth-and-vinyl interiors were phased out. Bucket seats were standard equipment with a bench seat optional. Molded rayon/nylon carpets were standard equipment as well.

The rear seats (shown on this fastback) aren't really meant to provide seating comfort for any trip other than a short hop to town. It's a very claustrophobic seating area, especially on the fastback.

The Mustang in its standard form provided the basics of transportation in a very pleasing body. The prospective customer was offered a large and ever increasing selection of options and encouraged to personalize his or her Mustang.

The 170 c.i. six-cylinder with its anemic performance was replaced by a larger 200 c.i. six-cylinder in the fall of 1964. Both were based on the original 144 c.i. six-cylinder that powered the 1960 Falcon. The 200 c.i. engine featured seven main bearings (four were used on the 144 and 170 c.i.) that provided additional strength. The 200 c.i. six-cylinder continued as the standard Mustang engine until 1970.

Here is a close-up of the wire wheel covers. Note the three-prong simulated knock-off.

One of the problems with this engine, at least from a performance point of view, was harmonic vibration. Vibrations travel from the front of the crankshaft to the flywheel, where they return to the front of the crank. This is normal with all engines. The problem with the 200 c.i. six-cylinder was that it did not have a vibration dampener to absorb the vibrations, so the bearings, timing gears, and even the flywheel could break when the engine was over-revved. The design of the integral intake manifold/head also severely limited engine breathing. Despite this, provided you didn't over-rev the 200 c.i., it was a hard engine to kill.

To provide more pep, a 164hp 260 c.i. V-8 and a 210hp 289 c.i. V-8 were optional. The 271hp 289 c.i. was available after June 1, 1964. By fall, the 260 c.i. was replaced with a two-barrel carbureted version of the 289 c.i. rated at 200hp. Although the 225hp Challenger 289 provided adequate performance with 0-60 mph times in the 8.5 second range and quarter-mile times of about 16.5 seconds, it could not be considered high-performance. For more power and acceleration, the 271hp 289 c.i. V-8 was the way to go.

All Mustangs had vertical and horizontal grille bars. This convertible has the optional simulated wheel covers. This Mustang looks great with the top down.

The 289 c.i. was one of Ford's best engines. The engine family was originally designed in 1958 as an answer to Chevrolet's highly successful small-block. It did not come into production until 1961, and then with only 221 c.i. It was not particularly successful and so was enlarged to 260 and then to 289 c.i. Unlike earlier Ford engines, this was a compact, light engine, weighing about 450 pounds complete. It featured lightweight thin-wall casting techniques, and with its 4.00 x 2.87 in. bore and stroke, it was conducive to high-rpm operation. The basic engine was in production until 1996.

The 271hp engine had a larger 480 cfm Autolite carburetor, versus the 470 cfm unit found on the 225hp 289. A higher compression ratio of 10.5:1 and a performance dual-point distributor further distinguished it. Internally, the engine used a mechanical camshaft that enabled it to rev higher and produce more power. To ensure reliability at a higher rpm, the 271hp 289 c.i. had screw-in rocker arm studs, special connecting rods with larger, stronger ⅜-inch rod bolts and a special harmonic balancer. The balancer, two inches wide versus one inch for other 289s, was designed to operate at engine speeds up to 7000 rpm. A low-restriction air cleaner topped off the engine and added some distinction. A special feature that made this Mustang special was a low-restriction dual exhaust system. Ford rated it at 271hp at 6000 rpm, but that was based on a gross rating. Measured by today's net rating, actual power was closer to 230-235 hp. Mandatory with this engine was a four speed manual transmission with either a 3.89:1 or 4.11:1 axle ratio in the larger nine-inch rear axle. The letter K designated the 271hp engine on the Mustang's VIN and soon, the engine was referred to as the K by knowledgeable enthusiasts.

The 271hp engine improved acceleration dramatically: 0–60 mph times in the mid-seven-second range and quarter-mile times in the high fifteens. Although these figures do not seem that impressive by today's standards, the subjective feeling was that this car was much faster than it really was. The high numerical axle ratio made this Mustang responsive and eager to accelerate. Downshifting and flooring it at the same time brought about considerable sensory input: You were pushed back into your seat as the nose of the car rose about six inches, while the engine screamed and the tires more often than not broke traction.

The 289 c.i two- and four-barrel engines were the most commonly found on the Mustang. Early engines were painted black from the factory with a gold air cleaner.

Here is a close-up of the styled steel wheels. Very handsome, indeed.

The 271hp engine had a special handling package that included stiffer springs and shocks, as well as 14 inch tires and wheels. Optional with the V-8s and suspension package were 5.90 x 15 Firestone Super Sport tires, but these were replaced with 6.95 x 14s by the fall of 1964.

The automatic transmission was not available with the K engine, but it was available on all other Mustang engines, as was a four-speed manual in place of the standard three-speed manual. Other important options included power brakes, manual

By far the most coveted Mustang interior was the Interior Décor Group or as it was called the Pony interior. Its claim to fame was the embossed Ponies on the seats. This interior also has the Rally Pac and air conditioning.

front disc brakes, power steering with a faster 22:1 ratio, limited-slip differential, styled steel wheels, under-dash air conditioning, and Rally Pac. The Rally Pac combined a clock and tachometer and was mounted on the steering column. A host of dealer-installed options were available in addition to a variety of trim and functional options.

Two significant options were made available in the early spring of 1965. The first was the Interior Decor Group, introduced in March 1965. This was essentially a luxury interior option with deluxe door panels, special seat upholstery with galloping pony inserts, a wood grained steering wheel, wood grained appliqués on the glove box door, and a special five-dial instrument cluster, as well as some trim differences. The all-important letter B indicated the Interior Decor Group on the body-side code on the warranty plate. Thus in 1965, the designations 65B, 63B, and 76B indicated the luxury interior, while the standard interior had the letter A. The Pony interior, as the luxury option was commonly called, did spruce up the inside.

The other option was the GT Equipment Group. Available on all three body styles, the GT Equipment Group enhanced the Mustang's appearance and also improved performance. It was available with either the 225hp or 271hp 289 c.i. and it included manual front disc brakes, handling package, quick-ratio steering, dual exhaust with chrome exhaust trumpets exiting through the rear valance panel, rocker panel stripes, GT emblems, and two fog lamps on each end of the grille opening. Inside, the standard instrument bezel was replaced with the five-dial version that housed

Notchback Mustangs were the most common Mustang; those equipped with the GT Equipment Group were quite rare.

Dual exhausts were part of the GT Equipment Group as were these exhaust trumpets.

gauges for fuel, temperature, speed, oil pressure, and amps. GTs equipped with the Pony interior got the same five-dial bezel, but with the walnut trim. Later in the model year, Ford made available the appearance items as dealer-installed accessories. The styled steel wheels and Rally Pac were not part of the GT Equipment Group but they do complement it and have become popular add-ons today.

This is the 271hp "K" engine. The Cobra valve covers are owner installed.

True GTs built from February 1965 through August 1965 had date codes from P through V on the warranty plates. Besides the date code on the warranty plate, other differences distinguished early 1965 Mustangs from later ones. The most obvious difference in the early 1965 models was the use of a generator, while Mustangs built after August used an alternator; wiring is different for each of these. The 170 c.i. six-cylinder engine was only available on the early cars. The passenger seat was not adjustable (although you'll find later Mustangs may also have this type of seat). On later cars, Allen screws held on window cranks and door handles. Early cars had a two-speed blower; later cars had a three-speed. A host of other minor differences existed as well.

Any Mustang looked better with the optional styled steel wheels such as this. The 1965 versions have a red center cap.

Compared to today's Mustangs, the 1965 is dated, but overall, you'll find that you can drive the car every day. The seats do not offer much lateral support and do not have any rake adjustment. The steering wheel is a bit on the large side when compared to modern ones as well. The dash is simple so you don't need a college degree to figure out how everything works. The heating and air-conditioning systems work just fine, but there is more interior noise at high speeds and the radio leaves a lot to be desired. You'll be surprised by how nicely and smoothly the engine idles and how responsive it is, even though the power steering is light and doesn't convey much road feel. Driving a 1965 convertible would get you noticed, though. There's no doubt about that.

The Mustang lettering on the front fenders was 4⅜ inches long on the early Mustangs; in the 1965 Mustangs, their length was increased to 5 inches.

SPECIALS

The Mustang got to pace the 1964 Indianapolis 500 race. In addition, 185 Indianapolis Pace Car replica hardtops were given to Ford dealers as prizes in the Green and Checkered Flag Contests. All 185 cars were powered by the 260 c.i. engine. Photo courtesy of Brad Bowling.

The rarest 1965 Mustangs are the Indianapolis 500 Pace Cars. Two 1964½ convertibles were used in the race itself. One was the official pace car and the other was a back-up car. There were also 35 convertibles given to the Indianapolis 500 dignitaries and festival board of directors. All were powered by 289 c.i., but the two pace cars came with the high performance 289 c.i. (K) and Borg-Warner transmissions. All pace cars were painted Pace Car White, which was different from the production Wimbledon White, with either red, white, or blue interiors. All these cars had the letter C as a color code, which also designated the color Honey Gold on 1965 Mustangs. Some of the festival cars are still in existence, while the two cars used in the race wait to be found.

Ford also built 185 Indianapolis Pace Car replica hardtops and gave them to Ford dealers as prizes in the Green and Checkered Flag Contests. All were equipped with the 260 c.i. V-8 and automatic transmission. They all were Pace Car White with a white and blue vinyl interior and had the Pace Car decals as well.

PROSPECTS

If you intend to restore a classic Mustang be wary of rust. I don't think there is a part on these cars that doesn't rust. Doors, fenders, rear quarters, rocker panels, torque-boxes, engine compartment, roof, floors—you name it, all are susceptible to rust. It's best to look for an original car with no rust. If this is not an option and you are looking at a restoration, make sure that you inspect the car thoroughly. Rust damage repaired with Bondo means that the rust will return, and soon. Stay away from total rust buckets as they will require major replacement of parts with salvaged original or after-market products. The huge investment of time, money, and skill will not be worth the effort except to the most dedicated enthusiast.

You may be asking, which Mustang would be the best value for the money for you? A brief look at the production figures for 1965 Mustangs will show that Ford built 680,989 cars. Of these, 501,965 were hardtops. The sheer weight of these numbers suggests that prices for hardtops, at least in the near future, should remain reasonable. If you are considering a restoration, a 1965 Mustang convertible may be the better buy. Assuming the cost of parts and labor is the same for all three body styles, you are better off investing in a convertible or a fastback. You will see greater appreciation with these.

Fiberfab was a company that mostly sold fiberglass bodies for Volkswagens during the 1960s. However, they did make a few bodies for the Mustang such as the one shown here.

Although convertibles were built in greater numbers than fastbacks (101,945 versus 77,079), they have appreciated faster due to demand. The 1965 Mustang convertible is a classic design, and I think you'll see continued appreciation in spite of the high production.

Probably the most desirable 1965 car would be the convertible GT with the 271hp 289 and the Pony interior, along with such niceties as the styled steel wheels and Rally Pac. GTs with the 225hp Challenger are also quite desirable. I think a white or red Mustang is especially attractive. In any case, all 1965 Mustangs are beautiful and desirable, and we can be thankful that for the most part they are still readily available and not prohibitively expensive.

2
1966 Mustang

PRODUCTION

63A 2dr fastback Standard	27,809
63B 2dr fastback Luxury	7,889
65A 2dr hardtop Standard	422,416
65B 2dr hardtop Luxury	55,938
65C 2dr hardtop bench seats	21,397
76A convertible	56,409
76B convertible Luxury	12,520
76C convertible bench seats	3,190
Total	607,568

Why change a good thing? This was the rationale that Ford applied in making the 1966 Mustang, as production lines hummed trying to keep up with all the demand. Clearly, the Mustang was a phenomenon that established a new niche in the marketplace and enjoyed no real competition. Chrysler's Barracuda never really caught on, and General Motors' answers to the Mustang, the Camaro and the Firebird, were still a good year away. Ford dealers cleaned up.

Those of us who grew up in the sixties remember it as an optimistic time. The Mustang with its fresh styling and spirited performance was the right car for a large group of people who found the typi-

The Mustang was virtually unchanged between 1965 and 1966.

The notchback Mustang was produced in record numbers, so there are plenty of them still around. This is to the advantage of the collector who doesn't quite have the resources to obtain a convertible or fastback.

cal Detroit sedan boring. The Mustang with its smaller dimensions and lighter weight felt like a nimble sports car by comparison.

The 1966 Mustang sold at a faster pace than the record set in 1965: 607,568 units in 12 months versus 559,451 for 1965, if you exclude the 1964½s.

The most noticeable style change was the floating horse in the front grille that gave the Mustang a cleaner look. On the sides, three chrome spires simulated a side scoop, but this ornament was deleted on the fastback and on all Mustangs that came with the GT package, as well as on those with the accent pinstripe. Other visual changes included standard rocker panel moldings (except on the fastback), a redesigned gas cap, and standard back-up lights (optional on 1965 Mustangs). For

This notchback has the GT Equipment Group option. It is exactly the same color as the plain notchback (see first photo above).

The GT Equipment Group, of which 25,517 were produced, looks best in a fastback.

Here's something you don't see everyday. About 20 such Mustangs were built—these had a retractable rather than a regular convertible top.

the interior, different upholstery patterns and colors were available, but the most significant addition was the use of the five-dial instrument bezel across the board for both V-8 and six-cylinder Mustangs.

The standard wheel cover was redesigned, while the optional styled steel wheels used a chrome trim ring. Standard wheels were 14x4.5 inches (with four lugs) on six-cylinder Mustangs and 14x5 inches on V-8s. Tire size was 6.95x14.

The standard engine was the 200 c.i. six-cylinder with the non-synchromesh three-speed manual transmission. Optional were the 200hp, 225hp, and 271hp 289 c.i. V-8s as seen in 1965. The Cruise-O-Matic automatic transmission was an option with the 271hp 289 c.i.

You'll note that true GTs did not have side ornamentation on the rear quarter panel.

Trunk space was never a strong point for Mustangs. Who cares!

This nice example of a Mustang was also a Coca Cola car. It's one of a few cars that were used by Coca Cola. Note the logo above the Mustang logo on the front fender.

The Coca Cola logo.

The GT Equipment Group was basically the same as that offered in 1965. The most obvious change was the use of a unique GT gas cap. The GTs, however, continued to use the horizontal grille bars, and thus closely resembled the 1965 models.

The Interior Decor Group, too, remained practically unchanged. For those so desiring it, a front bench seat was optional again, on hardtops and convertibles, but not on fastbacks or any Mustang

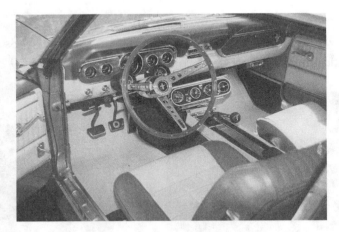

This interior, with its Interior Décor Group (Pony interior) also had a Rally Pac, air conditioning, optional steering wheel, and the standard five instrument pod. Perhaps a bit loud for today's customer, but still conveys a feeling of richness.

with the Interior Decor Group. Bench seats, although certainly rare, do not really contribute to a Mustang's value. They are more of an interesting curiosity.

SPECIALS

Sprint 200

To commemorate the one millionth Mustang sold, Ford released the Sprint 200 Option Group on the hardtop, convertible, and fastback. It consisted of the 200 six-cylinder engine, wire wheel covers, pinstripes, center console, and a chrome air cleaner with a Sprint 200 decal to dress up the engine compartment. The Sprint 200 Mustang was also a way for Ford to sell more six-cylinder Mustangs, since it was experiencing a shortage of the 289 c.i. V-8 engines. Many magazine advertisements promoted the Sprint 200. One target market was young women, with a lead line reading, "Six and the Single Girl."

The only way to tell a Sprint 200 from a regular Mustang is by noting the differences in equipment described here. Neither car has any special code or VIN number. One way to identify it is to see if the quarter panels are drilled open. A true Sprint 200 will not have the side ornamentation, so the attaching holes for it should not be drilled open. If you think that you are looking at a Sprint 200, you should look at the quarter panel from the inside to make sure.

The most popular engine for the 1966 Mustang was the 289.

There's plenty of room around the 200 c.i six-cylinder engine. Note the Export Brace on this example.

You won't find the word Mustang on this Mustang, because it was destined for Germany. As the word Mustang was someone else's property, all Mustangs destined for Germany were called T-5s.

T-5 Mustang

Also unique to the 1966 model year was the T-5 Mustang. The name Mustang had already been used by a manufacturer in Germany, so Ford renamed all Mustangs destined for Germany T-5. All Mustang emblems were removed, and T-5 emblems were used on both front fenders. This practice continued until 1979.

PROSPECTS

The recommendations for buying the 1966 Mustang are the same as those for the 1965 models. GT convertibles lead the way, followed by GT fastbacks. Production of Mustangs equipped with the 271hp 289 c.i. actually declined in 1966, thereby making these more desirable. As a group, the 1965-66 Mustangs represent the marque at its purest, but they are far from being rare. As for desirability, a slight edge goes to the 1965 Mustangs simply because they were the first.

3
1967 Mustang

PRODUCTION

65A 2dr hardtop	325,853
65B 2dr hardtop Luxury	22,228
65C 2dr hardtop bench seats	8,190
63A 2dr fastback	53,651
63B 2dr fastback Luxury	17,391
76A convertible	38,751
76B convertible Luxury	4,848
76C convertible bench seats	1,209
Total	472,121

Fortunately, Ford restyled the Mustang in 1967. As successful as the Mustang was, it still would have looked dated next to the Camaro and the Firebird, General Motors' entries into the pony car market.

When the design for the 1967 Mustang was finalized in early 1965, Ford did not know exactly what GM's answer to the Mustang would be. The Corvair clearly was no match, and it was obvious that GM would introduce something new, especially in light of the Mustang's incredible success.

Ford decided to stay with most of the successful original styling, while refining and improving the car.

31

The profile of the 1967 Mustang was the same as the earlier models, but it was larger. The quarter simulated brake scoop actually looked like a scoop, sort of. The optional styled steel wheels were the same as the 1965–66 versions, but with blue center caps.

No one could mistake the 1967 car for anything but a Mustang. It still looked like the original and retained the original's proportions, but became a bit fuller and rounder. The grille opening was enlarged, and this gave the 1967 car a meaner look. The 2+2 body, now a full fastback, looked sleeker than ever. All Mustangs got simulated scoops on the rear quarter panels, adding to the Mustang's performance image. The rear end treatment, while still using three tail lights per side, was changed considerably. The tail light panel was concave, simulating the spoilered look found on Ford's GT-40 endurance racers.

The wider track enabled Ford to improve the Mustang's ride and handling characteristics—a welcome improvement—while the enlarged engine compartment was now able to accommodate the big block 390 c.i. V-8. The change to a big block was a good thing because both GM Pony cars were designed for larger engines.

Even though the Mustang was larger, it still had the same proportions as the original.

Unfortunately, the 390 c.i. had poor front-to-rear weight distribution, and handling deteriorated. It lost the nimbleness of the 289 c.i. Mustangs. However, the 390 c.i. Mustang did not do so badly when compared with its competition.

The Mustang's grille opening was decidedly meaner looking.

The rear of the Mustang was different from previous models, as now the tail light panel was concave.

The fastback body style became a full fast-back. All three body styles had the rear quarter panel scoops.

One of the benefits of the 1967 Mustang is the larger engine compartment. The compartment enabled it to use the 390 c.i and larger engines.

The 289 c.i engine. Most Mustangs came with this engine.

The standard engine was the 200 c.i. six-cylinder with the three-speed manual. The only other transmission available with the six-cylinder was a three-speed automatic. Three 289 c.i. V-8s were available: a two-barrel carbureted rated at 200hp, a four-barrel carbureted V-8 rated at 225hp, and, appearing for the last time, the 271hp High Performance 289 (but only with the GT Equipment Group). All of these, except the 271hp 289 c.i., came with a three-speed manual transmission; a four-speed manual transmission and a three-speed automatic were optional.

Other driveline improvements included a slightly faster manual steering ratio, 25.3:1 (the power ratio was 20.3:1), and new front disc brakes were available with power assist.

For the serious enthusiast, the Competition Handling Package was available at a cost of $388.53. High cost limited the popularity of this option as it was only available with the GT Package. It included stiffened springs, Gabriel adjustable shocks, quick-ratio steering, a larger $^{15}/_{16}$-inch front anti-

This Group II Mustang was sold by Shelby American Inc. in 1967, and the car has been a racer since then. The sale included two bucket seats, a 37-gallon gas tank, two eight-inch front American Mags, two nine-inch rear American Mags, filler caps, an ignition box, and an electric fuel pump.

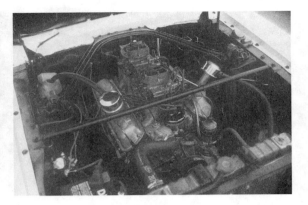

The engine of the Group II Mustang. It is a 289 c.i. K car and sports two Holley carburetors.

roll bar, limited-slip axle with a minimum 3.25:1 ratio and 15-inch steel wheels with wire wheel covers. The package was a worthwhile addition with the big 390 c.i. engine.

Major option groups included the Interior Decor Group without pony seat inserts and, of course, the GT Equipment Group, available only on V-8 Mustangs. It included grille-mounted fog lamps, power front disc brakes, dual exhausts with chrome quad outlets (excluded with the 200hp 289), and rocker panel stripes with the GT or GT/A (for automatic) emblem. There were also F70xI4 whitewall tires and a GT pop-open gas cap, as well as a handling package that consisted of firmer springs and shocks, and a larger front anti-roll bar.

This is another Group II racer raced by Shelby.

An Exterior Decor Group was also available for the first time. It included a hood with rear-facing louvers that also housed turn signal indicators, wheel-well moldings, rear deck moldings on convertibles and hardtops, and a pop-open gas cap. Other options and improvements included air conditioning with outlets built into the dash, convertible tops that used a folding glass rear window, cruise control, a tilt-away steering wheel, and wider styled steel wheels.

A 1967 Mustang GT fastback.

The 1967 Mustang was a better car, but competition from GM hurt sales. The Mustang still outsold all competitors combined, but the Mustang would no longer dominate the market in the same way.

PROSPECTS

The 1967 Mustangs are less expensive to acquire; again, convertible GTs lead the way in appreciation. K engine production hit a low with 472 units, so you are more likely to find a Mustang with the regular 289 or the 390 c.i. V-8. Get one with the 390 c.i. V-8 if you can.

You'll enjoy your Mustang more if you find one with air conditioning and the Interior Decor Group.

4
1968 Mustang

PRODUCTION

63A 2dr fastback	33,585
63B 2dr fastback Deluxe	7,661
63C 2dr fastback bench seats	1,079
63D 2dr fastback Deluxe bench seats	256
65A 2dr hardtop	233,472
65B 2dr hardtop Deluxe	9,009
65C 2dr hardtop bench seats	6,113
65D 2dr hardtop Deluxe bench seats	853
76A 2dr convertible	22,037
76B 2dr convertible Deluxe	3,339
Total	317,404

428CJ Mustang

2dr fastback	2,097
2dr hardtop	221
2dr convertible	552
Total	2,870

California GT/CS

2dr hardtop	4,117

This is a six-cylinder car with stock hub caps, but it is a 1968 convertible, and that makes all the difference.

Add the GT Equipment Group and the Mustang now has some pizzazz, even if it doesn't have the big 428 engine.

The 1968 Mustang received minor grille and trim modifications to set it off from the 1967. There were also some minor mechanical changes made in order to comply with government safety rules. The most significant of these was a collapsible steering column. Other more significant visual changes included deletion of the horizontal grille bars and of the simulated side scoops, and the use of side marker lights in the front and back.

This is the basic Mustang interior for 1968.

Ford gave the interior a new steering wheel design and different upholstery patterns, and for the first time the rearview mirror was affixed directly on the windshield. The Interior Decor Group was distinguished by the use of wood grain appliqués on the dash and doors and by the use of a wood grained steering wheel.

Many options were grouped together. The Sports Trim Group consisted of the wood grained dash, knitted vinyl bucket seat inserts on hardtops and fastbacks, wheel well moldings, a two-toned louvered hood, and argent (a dull silver)-styled steel wheels with E70x14 Wide Oval whitewalls for V-8 Mustangs. The two-toned hood, available separately as well, tended to give a plain-Jane Mustang a performance look. The Protection Group of options included color-keyed rubber floor mats, door-edge guards, and chrome license plate frames. For the GT Group, the Reflective Group included reflective GT stripes and paint on the styled wheels.

The GT Equipment Group changed, with the addition of a C-stripe that followed the bodyside contour. This was an adaptation of the stripe that Ford had used on its long-distance racing Ford GT-

A hardtop with a black vinyl roof and the GT Equipment Group.

40s. However, side stripes like those offered in 1967 could be substituted. The familiar fog lights remained, but the light bar between them was removed. The lights were mounted directly on the grille. GT emblems on each front fender, a GT pop-open gas cap, and GT letters on the hubcaps identified the package visually.

Heavy-duty suspension components remained unchanged from 1967. Power front disc brakes became optional, but were mandatory when the larger 390 c.i. was ordered. The dual exhaust system with its chrome quad tips was standard on all GT engines. However, only 4V (four-barrel carburetor) engines were available with the GT package. F70x14 WSW Firestone Wide Oval tires on six-inch-wide steel rims were also standard with this package. The 14x6 inch styled steel wheels that were part of the GT Equipment Group were either painted argent or chrome plated, and both used chrome trim rings and hubcaps with large GT letters. The 390 c.i. engine also came with chrome engine components (chrome valve covers, air cleaner lid, and oil filler cap).

The 390 c.i. engine was still the biggest engine you could get in a Mustang, at least in the beginning of the year. Later on, the brawny 428CJ was available and this allowed the driver to spin those wheels at will.

Engine selection was a bit more complicated than before. The standard engine was the 200 c.i. six-cylinder. Although both four-barrel 289s were deleted, the two-barrel carburetor version, now rated at 195hp, continued until it was replaced by a two-barrel carburetor 302 c.i. by mid-year. The highest rated small-block was now a 302 c.i., basically a stroked 289 c.i., rated at 230hp. It used a hydraulic cam

This is a beautiful Mustang GT.

From every angle, it looks great.

Chapter 4

The hottest engine in the GT was the 390 c.i.
Notice how this engine has been restored to the
fullest extent possible with various factory-scribed
marks. It's almost an art.

You'll note that this Mustang GT has a dual
exhaust system. The dual exhaust system only
came with Mustangs that had a four-barrel carburetor.

and a smallish 470 cfm Autolite four-barrel carburetor. Interestingly, the four-barrel carburetor 302
c.i. lasted only one year, and after that, you had to wait until 1983 if you wanted to buy a Mustang
with a four-barrel carburetor 302 (excluding the Boss 302).

The big 390 c.i. continued unchanged, but was now rated at 325 hp. A total of 10,650 Mustangs
got this engine while 733 were built with the 390 c.i. two-barrel engine, rated at 295hp.

The largest engine available was a hydraulic cam 427 rated at 390hp at 5600 rpm. The 427 c.i.,
however, was never available during the 1968 model run, although it was advertised as being
available.

SPECIALS

Cobra-Jet

On April 1,1968, Ford introduced the 428 Cobra-Jet engine as an option on fastback, hardtop, and
convertible Mustangs, to counter criticism that the Mustang couldn't hold its own against more powerful competitors. The line-up included the Cobra-Jet Mustangs. This engine was more reasonable
in cost, offered excellent street performance, and thus was attractive to the enthusiast.

A Cobra-Jet Mustang was more than just an engine option. The lower front suspension shock towers were strengthened. Both a functional Ram-Air induction system and revised rear suspension

This Mustang looks like a real sleeper—few would expect it to be as valuable as it is. The only give-away is the hood scoop (and how many people know to look for that?). Actually, it is one the 50 pre-production 428CJs that were supposed to be drag-raced.

Even from the back it's pretty plain, compared to a GT. This particular car was purchased from Tasca Ford, a renowned Ford dealer who did a lot of racing in the 1960s, and the original owner still owns the car.

This is the 428CJ engine that was used in the pre-production cars. It featured an aluminum intake manifold and absolutely no options at all—no power brakes, power steering, or radio.

shock absorber mounting for four-speed cars were included. By staggering the shocks, one in front of the axle and the other behind it, wheel hop during hard acceleration was largely eliminated. This was not a Ford exclusive; the Camaro also had staggered shocks in 1968. The Ram-Air induction system was also good for a 0.2 second improvement in quarter-mile times.

The 428CJ, as the engine was known, was available with either a four-speed manual or a C-6 automatic transmission. Standard axle ratio was 3.50:1, while 3.91:1 or 4.30:1 ratios were optional for even more acceleration. On this Mustang, a black hood stripe covered the hood scoop and cowl, and the GT Equipment Group was mandatory.

The 428CJ engine was basically a production 428 c.i. fitted with 427 c.i. Low Riser cylinder heads. The heads, however, used intake ports that were slightly larger, similar in size to those found on the Medium Riser 427 c.i. The camshaft was identical to the one in

The regular production 428CJ Mustangs were all GT's.

Unlike the plain pre-production Mustangs, the 428CJs could be had with most Mustang options.

The scoop, used with the 428CJ, was functional. It would also be used in 1969–70 Mustangs as well.

the Low Riser and 390 GT engines, but a larger 735 cfm Holley carburetor was mounted on a cast-iron copy of the 428 c.i. Police Interceptor intake manifold. The 428CJ also used an oil pan windage tray. It was rated at 335hp at 5200 rpm, which was obviously on the low side.

Instead of the Firestone Wide Ovals, the 428CJ Mustangs got Goodyear Polyglas F70x14 tires mounted on the GT styled steel wheels. These were the best street tires available at the time and made their debut on this Mustang. The 428CJ Mustangs also came with 31 spline rear axles. According to drag racing magazines, the 428CJ was able to crank out quarter-mile times in the low- to mid-13-second range; other magazines recorded times in the low- to mid-14s.

Obviously appealing to drag-oriented customers, the cars supplied to hot rod magazines for testing were specially tuned by Ford, a common practice at the time. So-called test cars usually were delivered on company trailers for testing, with several engineers to ensure that they functioned properly.

Some of these test cars were actually pre-production 428CJ Mustangs. Every one of these 50 cars were somewhat different than the regular production 428CJs. They did not come with disc brakes, power steering, staggered rear shocks, front shock tower bracing, argent wheels, or a radio, and the engine sported an aluminum intake manifold. The production 428CJs came with the cast iron copy. If you know Ford engines at all, you know that the intake manifold is a real heavyweight, weighing about 100 lbs.

A total of 2,097 fastbacks, 221 hardtops, and 552 convertibles with the 428CJ were built. Any that are left are a collector's dream.

One of the more popular Regional Specials, at least in terms of numbers (4,117), is the California Special. It used many of the GT and Shelby styling features.

From the back it is evident that the Shelby Mustang rear end is used. The spoiler on the rear incorporated Thunderbird taillights. Actually, there were some plans for bringing out a hardtop Shelby, but it never happened.

Regional Specials

Several specialty Mustangs were sold during 1968. One was the Mustang Sprint with a special option package available on both six-cylinder and V-8 Mustangs. On the six-cylinder cars, the package included GT side stripes, a pop-open gas cap, and full wheel covers. The V-8s had in addition the Wide Oval tires on styled steel wheels and the GT fog lamps.

More significant was the California Special. Available mostly in California, the GT/CS was a trim package for the hardtop Mustang that used many GT and Shelby Mustang styling features. The most obvious was the Shelby rear deck lid with integral spoiler and sequential taillights. Shelby side scoops were also used, but these were nonfunctional. A blacked-out front grille without any Mustang emblems used rectangular Lucas or Marchal fog lamps. The GT/CS also got a distinctive side stripe that began at the front fender and ended at the side scoop. Wheels were the styled steel wheels without the GT identification. The GT/CS could be had with any regular production Mustang engine. Production was 4,117.

Here is something you don't see everyday. It's a 428CJ Mustang that is also a High Country Special.

Another limited edition Mustang, the High Country Special, was essentially the GT/CS but sold through Colorado dealers. It differed from the GT/CS in that the California Special identification was deleted, and the GT/CS on the side scoop was replaced with a High Country Special decal. High Country Specials

A High Country Special has two stickers affixed on the rear scoops. Without these stickers, the car is really a California Special.

The High Country Special identification sticker.

were available in Colorado from 1966 on, but the only thing special about them were the two badges located on the front fenders. Other specials offered in 1968 included the Sunshine Special and the Nebraska Big Red.

With all the different specials and option groups, it was evident that Ford was widening the Mustang's appeal and marketing it to specific niches. This strategy continued through 1970.

PROSPECTS

The 1968½ Cobra-Jet is the most sought-after 1968 Mustang, followed by the GTs. If you can't find one of these, the GT convertibles and fastbacks with the 390 c.i. engine are good alternatives.

There isn't much difference between the 1967 and 1968 Mustangs in terms of prices. It is only a matter of taste. Those favoring the 1967 car probably notice that they have many visual features that are common to the 1965-66 Mustangs, such as the optional wheels, GT stripes, and the small-block engines. The 1968 Mustangs have features that are found on the 1969 Mustangs: styled steel wheels, more blatant striping, and blacked-out hoods—and more emphasis on performance.

Rust is still the major problem with 1967–68 Mustangs. Again, unless you are looking at a big-engine convertible GT, you are better off not restoring a badly rusted-out car.

As performance became a more dominant theme, the 390/428CJ Mustangs were abused at some point and many were probably modified as well. Look at these cars closely.

5
1969 Mustang

PRODUCTION

63A 2dr fastback	56,022
63B 2dr fastback deluxe	5,958
63C 2dr fastback Mach 1	72,458
65A 2dr hardtop	118,613
65B 2dr hardtop deluxe	5,210
65C 2dr hardtop bench seats	4,131
65D 2dr hardtop deluxe bench seats	504
65E 2dr hardtop Grande	22,182
76A convertible	11,307
76B convertible deluxe	3,439
Total	299,824

Specials

Boss 302	1,628
Boss 429	859 (includes 2 Boss Cougars)

The year 1969 was an important one for the Mustang. Despite significant restyling, you could easily trace the car's origins, because it retained all of the original Mustang styling cues. The result was
lower, sleeker, and meaner. While the car grew in size, it maintained the 108 inch wheelbase. The
restyle was particularly effective on the fastback, now called the SportsRoof, and all performance

45

All the hoopla in 1969 was for this car—the Mach 1. It's ready to take off!

Mustangs were based on it. In fact, over forty-four percent of all Mustangs sold that year were fastbacks.

Of course, if you look at the 2005 and later Mustangs, you're bound to notice the resemblance to the 1969 Mustang, especially from the front. It's the new retro look and after 36 years, it is still popular!

Most of the interior and exterior dimensions grew in 1969, although not dramatically. More importantly, all Mustangs were lowered 0.5 inch on the suspension, and the windshield rake was increased by 2.2 degrees. This translated into a 150–175 lbs weight increase depending on the model.

The roofline on the SportsRoof was lowered by 0.9 inch. The side sculpturing was eliminated for a cleaner, smoother look, but the most important visual changes were made on the front grille and the rear tail treatment on the SportsRoof. The revised front grille was enlarged and used four four-inch headlights for a decidedly aggressive look. The SportsRoof also received simulated side scoops and a spoiler on the rear, similar to the Shelby Mustangs but less pronounced.

This is an interesting 1969 convertible as it has certain Mach 1 options and not others.

The restyled interior effectively carried the racing theme inside, especially on cars that featured the Deluxe Interior Decor Group (the Mach 1, Boss 429, and Grande). This package had simulated wood-grain appliqués on the instrument panel, doors, and con-

The wheels are optional and the exhaust outlets indicate a four-barrel engine.

The most interesting option is the grille—it is chromed from the factory. A few such grilles were made, but later it was withdrawn.

sole. Cars with this interior also had a round clock on the passenger side of the dash panel; it looked nice, but was difficult for the driver to read. The Deluxe Interior Decor Group was optional only on the SportsRoof and convertibles.

The smallest V-8 available on the 1969 Mustang is the 302 c.i. two-barrel engine.

While we're discussing interiors, there was also the Interior Decor Group, that used Comfortweave upholstery on the seats, molded door panels with wood appliqué, a deluxe three-spoke Rim-Blow steering wheel, and a remote rectangular mirror on the driver's side. High-back bucket seats, first seen on 1969 Mustangs, were available with either interior option.

The standard Mustang interior is shown on this convertible, although it also does have the optional Rim Blow steering wheel.

If you ordered a tachometer, you also got a different arrangement of the dash pods for the driver's side. The tachometer took the place of the standard fuel and temperature gauges on the large right side pod. The temperature gauge was then relocated to the far left small pod (which displaced the standard alternator gauge), and the necessary fuel gauge took the place of the standard oil pressure gauge on the far right small pod. Unfortunately, Ford did not retain the alternator and oil pressure gauges, as it had done with the Shelby interior.

The options list included some new items for 1969. The Exterior Decor Group consisted of rocker panel moldings and wheel-well and rear end moldings, as well as the basic five-spoke full wheel cover. Additional interior lights were an option. Intermittent windshield wipers, power ventilation, and radial tires were all new 1969 options.

The standard engine was still the 200 c.i. six-cylinder with a three-speed manual transmission. The three-speed manual was standard equipment on all engines up to the 351 c.i. four-barrel carburetor. The three-speed Cruise-O-Matic

Shown here is the Interior Decor Group, which was standard equipment on the Mach 1.

47

automatic transmission was optional on all engines. A larger six-cylinder engine measuring 250 c.i. was also available. The larger engine included air conditioning if you desired it, but the 200 c.i. version didn't.

There were other engines to be had on the Mach 1. The base engine was the 351W with the two-barrel carburetor. Other engines were the 351W four-barrel and the 390.

The smallest optional V-8 was a two-barrel carburetor version of the 302 c.i. rated at 210hp. Next in line were two versions of a new engine. The 351W was basically a stretched 302 c.i. Increasing the stroke of the 302 c.i. to 3.5 inches raised the block's height by one inch. At the same time, the crank journals were resized, resulting in an engine that had no interchangeability with the 289/302 engines, save for the cylinder heads. The heads, by the way, had slightly larger ports. The engine was built at Ford's Windsor plant, and so came to be known as the 351W.

Ford's other 351, the 351C built in Cleveland, was available on Mustangs from 1970 through 1974. The 351W was the only 351 c.i. V-8 that was available on the 1969 Mustangs. The 351W was rated at 250hp with a 350 cfm two-barrel Autolite carburetor and 290hp with a 470 cfm four-barrel carburetor. It was a good design with a strong bottom end; unfortunately, restrictive porting and valves for an engine of that size limited performance to low- to mid-range rpm. In stock or modified form, a comparably modified 351C will run circles around the 351W.

The old 390 c.i. was still available to bridge the gap between the 351 c.i. and the 428 c.i. The same 428 Cobra-Jet engine introduced in the 1968½ Cobra-Jet Mustang was the top engine option but there were also three other versions available.

The hottest engine in a Mach 1 was the 428CJ with Ram Air and the Shaker hood scoop. Only the Shaker was available with the 428CJ.

The first, the 428CJ, was available without a functional hood scoop. An additional $133 got you the second version, known as the 428 Cobra-Jet Ram-Air with the unique Shaker hood scoop. The scoop incorporated a trap door that let outside cool air enter the air cleaner whenever the gas pedal was floored. It worked well, as quarter-mile times usually improved by two mph and 0.2 seconds. The Shaker scoop, connected directly to the engine, moved along with any engine movement and this really gave a Mustang equipped with this engine the edge in 1969.

The third version was known as the 428 Super Cobra Jet Ram-Air (428SCJ). It came with the Shaker scoop but had some additional important features. The 428SCJ was available only when a 3.91:1 or 4.30:1 axle ratio was ordered, and it differed mainly from the other versions because the engine had special cap screw connecting rods, similar to the 427 Le Mans rods. These were much stronger and accordingly gave more reliable higher engine rpm. Part of the SCJ pack-

The hottest engine in a Mach 1 was the 428CJ with Ram Air and the Shaker hood scoop. Only the Shaker was available with the 428CJ.

age included an engine oil cooler, mounted in front of the radiator. This was good for a 30-degree drop in engine oil temperature, again a measure to increase reliability. Ford did not issue a different engine code for the SCJ, but any 428CJ-R Mustangs with the axle code V for 3.91:1 or W for 4.30:1 were SCJs.

Ford used the 1969 model year to introduce two special Mustangs designed to appeal to a segment of the market looking for luxury as well as performance. The first of these was the Mustang Grande. The Grande was a luxury version of the Mustang hardtop designed to compete with Mercury's Cougar and the luxury versions of the Camaro and the Firebird. On the outside, the Grande got wire wheel covers, dual color-keyed mirrors, a two-tone paint stripe, wheel well rocker panels, rear deck moldings, and Grande script lettering on each C-pillar.

An interesting special is the 600 Limited Edition. Not much is known about it other than the decals on each fender, and that it also had the six-cylinder engine.

The interior was the Deluxe Decor Group plus a special insulation package that added 55 lbs to the Mustang's weight. This insulation consisted of thick, heavy sound-deadening pads underneath the carpets. You could order the Grande with any of the Mustang engines.

During 1969, another special Mustang, called the Mustang E, was introduced for the frugal segment of the market. The E came with the 250 c.i. six-cylinder coupled to an automatic transmission with a high-stall torque converter, and it used a low numerical axle ratio, 2.33:1. A rare bird, the Mustang E was available only on the SportsRoof Mustang body.

Mach 1

Ford stylists went all-out for the Mach 1. Actually, it's a pretty good-looking car. Today's 2005 Mustang GT borrows considerably from the 1969 Mach 1.

A very significant entry for the 1969 model year was the new Mach 1, because it took the place of the GT as the premier performance Mustang. Stripes, scoops, and spoilers accentuated the image of a street racer and promised incredible performance. The hood was painted flat black with body color trim, and had a simulated hood scoop similar to the one on the 1968½ Cobra-Jet Mustang. NASCAR-style hood pin latches (an option) enhanced the race car image; reflective side and tail stripes coordinated with the body color; a chrome pop-open gas cap and chrome styled steel wheels added to the package. The four-barrel carburetor engines got the usual chrome quad-tipped dual exhaust system. The handling suspension, now called the Competition Suspension, consisted of heavier springs and shocks, a larger diameter front anti-roll bar, and staggered rear shocks for the four-speed Mach 1.

The Mach 1 also had some industry firsts. The body-colored racing mirrors, standard on the Mach 1, have since been widely copied, as has the Shaker hood scoop that came with the 428CJ Ram-Air engine. In 1970, the Firebird Trans Am got a Shaker-type scoop, as did Chrysler's Barracuda and Challenger. The Shaker hood scoop was also optional on the 351 and 390 c.i. engines.

The standard engine for the Mach 1 was the 351 two-barrel carbureted V-8, with the other V-8s optional. Performance with the big 428 c.i. was similar to that of the 1968½ Cobra-Jet Mustang with quarter-mile times reported in the high-13- to low-14-second range. As you would expect, the 428CJ Ram-Air engine was the most desirable engine.

No Sport Slats, no rear wing, no Magnum 500 wheels, and no front spoiler—many current owners have installed these options, as the Mach 1 did not come with these Boss 302 options.

Considering tire technology in the late sixties, these were excellent tires, especially since the 428CJ was known for its tremendous low-end torque. On the other hand the F70x14 tires were just not enough tire. The big-block Mach 1 would have been better off with the wider F60x15 Goodyear tires that were standard equipment on the Bosses, and came with most 1969 Shelby Mustangs.

The Mach 1 has been called the Supercar of the masses because it was hard to resist the styling. Production levels were kept high to satisfy demand. For the Mach 1, Ford chose to include a particularly nice feature, the Deluxe Interior Group: a Rim-Blow steering wheel, console, special high-back bucket seats, and the 55 lbs insulation package. Previous GT Mustangs and performance Mustangs came with the basic interior, and lack of fine interior equipment had detracted from the total GT concept.

Ford built 72,450 Mach I cars in 1969, and while 13,193 of the 1969 Mustangs came with a version of the 428CJ, quite likely ninety-five percent of these were Mach 1 cars. As prices for Shelby and Boss Mustangs have been rising strongly in the past few years, the 428 Mach 1 has become a viable alternative.

Not to be forgotten, the Mustang GT was still available in 1969, catering to those who were put off

Shown here are Mach 1 standard and optional features: the Shaker hood scoop, an Interior Decor Group door panel, the styled steel wheels, and the Sport mirrors.

Shown here are two hood scoops signifying which engine the Mustang was equipped with. The options were the 390 c.i. and the 428CJ without Ram Air.

by the Mach 1's flash. Engine availability was identical to that of the Mach 1. The GT Equipment Group followed tradition to the end and was available on all three Mustang body styles. The option consisted of rocker panel stripes, a GT gas cap, styled steel wheels with GT identification, NASCAR-style hood-pin latches, dual exhausts with chrome quad outlets (on four-barrel engines), and heavy duty suspension.

Only 4,973 GTs were sold. But I have seen some interesting combinations, such as a GT convertible with a 428CJ Ram-Air and the deluxe interior.

A point to remember is that all 1969 Mustangs, including the Mach 1s, will have drum brakes as standard equipment. If you are interested in one of the more powerful Mustangs, you should try to get a car that has the power front disc brake option, simply for safety's sake. Power steering is nice, too.

Boss 302

Ford enthusiasts had been calling for a balanced car that could provide not only good acceleration but good handling and braking as well. The only such car on the market in 1968 was the Camaro Z-28, which sold 7,199 units; predictions were that 1969 sales would hit 20,000 units. The Z-28 also won 10 out of the 13 races in the 1968 Trans-Am series. This was an important loss for Ford because it was heavily involved in the Sports Car Club of America (SCCA) Trans-Am series, in which pony cars raced with factory support. More importantly, Ford had won the series in 1966 and 1967, so being trounced by Chevrolet didn't sit well. Ford engineers responded by developing the Boss 302 Mustang engine to replace the unreliable Tunnel Port 302. For the Ford teams to be able to use the engine, SCCA rules required that at least 1,000 cars with this engine be sold to the public, and the Boss 302 Mustang was born. It had originally been intended to be called the "Mustang

Trans Am" but since Pontiac had the rights to that name, Ford decided to call the new Mustang a Boss 302 as well.

The Boss 302 was based on the 1969 SportsRoof body, but without the simulated side body scoops. Ford wanted to produce a car that purists could appreciate, so anything that wasn't functional was eliminated. Visually, the Boss 302 was daring; it had a purposeful, racy look. The hood was blacked out, as was the area around the outside headlights, the rear deck area, and the rear tail light panel. A large C-stripe with Boss 302 lettering decorated the sides. Exterior color choice was limited to just four colors: Wimbledon White, Bright Yellow, Calypso Coral, and Acapulco Blue.

The Boss 302 was also another special car for 1969. It didn't have the side scoops that other SportsRoofs had, but it certainly had lots of black paint.

The Boss 302 also used a front spoiler designed to keep the nose of the car down at high speeds. Popular Boss 302 options were the rear wing and the rear window slats. The adjustable wing was designed to control the rear at high speeds, while the slats just enhanced the appearance of the car. Although roof slats originally were seen in a Corvair prototype in 1963 and on the Lamborghini Miura, it was the Boss 302 that popularized them.

Like the Boss 429, the exhaust system did not have any chrome extensions on it. The rear Sport Slats and rear wing were both new for 1969. Many enthusiasts, Boss 429, Mach 1, and SportsRoof owners are under the misunderstanding that these were available from the dealer in 1969. Never mind that there weren't any to be had.

Part of the Boss 302's visual impact turned on the standard argent-painted Magnum 500 wheels (chrome was optional) mounting the large F60x15 Goodyear Polyglas tires. These were the best street tires available at the time. With these tires, the Boss 302 was able to generate high cornering speeds that led to the failure of front-suspension control-arm mounting points on Boss 302 prototypes. For this reason, all Boss 302s were equipped with reinforced shock towers, along with larger spindles to handle the extra cornering loads.

Unlike other performance Mustangs, the Boss 302 was a complete package with a limited number of options. The only engine available was the Boss 302, mated to a wide ratio four-speed manual transmission. A 3.50:1 rear axle ratio was standard, with 3.91:1 and 4.30:1 optional. Additional standard features were front disc brakes, quick-ratio steering (16:1) with power assist recommended, staggered rear shocks, and color-keyed rearview mirrors. The fenders were radiused to clear the wide F60x15 tires that can be used to identify a Boss 302. Most Boss 302s came with the standard Mustang interior, although the deluxe interior was optional.

There's no doubt that what made the Boss 302 special was the engine. The block was a strengthened version of the production 302 block, with four-bolt main caps. It used a forged steel crankshaft with forged connecting rods that were the same as those found on the old High Performance 289. All this was done to ensure reliability.

The reason for the excellent power output was the redesigned cylinder heads. These had extremely large intake and exhaust ports. Canted valves measured

The Boss 302 engine. It's a little gem.

2.23 inches on the intake and 1.72 inches on the exhaust and adjustable rocker arms. In comparison, the High Performance 289 had valves measuring 1.78 inches on the intake and 1.44 inches on the exhaust. An aluminum high-rise intake manifold with a large Holley 780 cfm Holley four-barrel carburetor provided induction on the Boss. A subdued mechanical lifter camshaft was used, as was a dual-point distributor and dual exhaust system. Very little else was really necessary to convert the Boss 302 into a full-blown race engine.

One of the few racing Boss 302s that has survived. Ford was heavily involved in Trans Am racing and just barely came second in the 1969 series. This particular Boss 302 was driven by Peter Revson.

To ensure reliability on the street, Ford installed a rev-limiter, which stopped the engine from revving over 6150 rpm. The engine was good to 7000 rpm, with an occasional burst to 7500 rpm. Even with the rev limiter, the Boss 302 was rated at 290 hp at 5800 rpm. Obviously underrated, the Boss 302 could cover the quarter-mile in the high-14-second range and make 0–60 mph times under seven seconds.

The Boss 302 was enthusiastically received; finally a Mustang could handle with the best, and had

"Supercar" acceleration to boot. It provided Ford with a base for a better Trans-Am racer, and although it came in second in the 1969 series, the Boss 302 took the 1970 series.

You can expect these beauties to appreciate, although they still don't have quite the stature of a Shelby Mustang. The Boss 302 is a true thoroughbred, only lacking the magic of the Shelby name.

One thing to watch out for in a Boss 302 is the stock pistons. These tended to crack somewhere between 10,000 and 30,000 miles; a rebuild was then needed. If you find an original Boss 302 with less than 30,000 miles on the odometer, plan to rebuild the engine, unless of course you're going to trailer the car.

Boss 429

Many consider the Boss 429 to be the ultimate Mustang, and I must admit that I am partial to them, after having owned two.

When it first was available for sale, the Boss 429 was kept pretty low-key, rarely seen, and not really promoted. Today, of course, the situation has changed dramatically.

In many ways, the Boss 429 was similar to the early 1965-66 Shelby Mustangs. They were both built on a special production line, and both received many expensive, unique hand-built modifications. It was more than just a case of dropping a big (really big) engine in the Mustang chassis.

As 1960s cars go, the Boss 429 was rather sedate looking—until you opened the hood.

Only a small front fender decal identified the car as the Boss 429.

The Boss 429 Mustang came into being to satisfy NASCAR rules. Ford needed to satisfy the sanctioning body that regulated stock car racing, a most important area of Ford's racing program in the 1960s. To stay competitive with Chrysler's 426 Hemi, Ford developed its own version of the Hemi engine, but with some innovations. NASCAR rules stated that if Ford wanted to race this engine, at least 500 cars with the engine had to be built and sold to the general public. It would have seemed more logical to install this new engine in the larger Torino intermediate, but it was decided on the Mustang instead.

Ford instituted a crash program to develop and build the necessary 500 cars. The Boss 429 was no ordinary engine. Being physically large, the engine necessitated enlargement and modification of the Mustang's engine compartment. Ford subcontracted this to Kar Kraft, who also built many of Ford's race and experimental cars.

In 1969, SportsRoof Mustangs that normally would have received the 428SCJ engine were shipped to Kar Kraft. There the spring towers were moved outward and reinforced. At the same time, the suspension mounting points were relocated by lowering and moving them outward by one inch, much in the way the suspension of the all-out race Boss 302 Mustang had been modified. Then the complete engine and transmission combination was lowered as a unit into the car.

Externally, the Boss 429 retained the simulated side scoops of the SportsRoof Mustang and also used the color-keyed side view mirrors. Like the Boss 302, the Boss 429 used a front spoiler, although it was slightly shallower as the car sat lower. The only other visual clues were the fender decals and the large hood scoop. Wheels were chrome Magnum 500s, using the Goodyear F60x15 tires. Because the Boss 429 preceded the Boss 302 by about two months, the Boss 429 has the distinction of being the first vehicle to have these tires. Only one interior was available: the deluxe interior with console, an 8000 rpm tachometer, a Rim-Blow steering wheel, and 55 lbs of sound-deadening insulation.

The hood scoop was pretty big—the largest that Ford made.

Standard Boss 429 features included engine oil cooler, trunk-mounted battery, power disc brakes, power steering, close-ratio four-speed manual transmission, staggered rear shocks, manual choke, and manually operated hood scoop. Although the 4.30:1 Detroit Locker rear was optional, most cars came with the 3.91:1 Traction Lok rear. The Boss 429 had the heaviest springs ever installed in a production Mustang. It had a $^{15}/_{16}$

inch front anti-roll bar, and was the first to have a rear anti-roll bar, in this case measuring ¾ inch. The dual exhaust system, identical to the 428CJ system, did not have the chrome exhaust tips, and most Boss 429s came with the plain gas cap.

Boss 429s were available in six colors: Raven Black, Black Jade, Royal Maroon, Candy Apple Red, Wimbledon White, and Blue.

The 429 engine was labeled 429CJ-R HO on the driver's door, but it has also been called the Blue Crescent 429, the Shotgun 429, Twisted Hemi 429, and, of course, the Boss 429. Although the Mustang received many specialized parts, it is the engine that made this Mustang unique. In simple terms, aluminum cylinder heads were mated to the cast-iron 429 engine block. On closer examination, the differences between the Boss 429 and other engines became clear.

The cylinder block, while similar in appearance to other 429/460 blocks, was cast from nodular iron and therefore much harder. It also had a unique four-gallery oiling system, four-bolt main caps, and thick cylinder walls that could be overboard by 0.160 inch. The crankshaft was forged steel, as were the rods, and the engine used 10.5:1 compression pistons. A strong bottom end was necessary to cope with the extra power the aluminum cylinder heads produced. They featured modified (Crescent) hemispherical combustion chambers, extremely large intake and exhaust ports, and valves that were among the largest of any production engine ever.

It's interesting how well the Boss 429 handles. To get the engine in the engine compartment, the engineers moved the front suspension and also used a rear anti-roll bar, the first in a Mustang.

Intake valves measured 2.28 in. while exhausts were 1.90 in., arranged in a crossflow pattern to enhance upper-rpm performance. The Hemi design was known for its strong mid- to upper-rpm performance; Ford tried to combine the strong low-end performance of the wedge combustion chamber design with the high-end of the Hemi.

Another interesting feature was the dry-deck method of mounting the heads on the block; no conventional head gasket was used. Instead, copper O-rings sealed the cylinders while rubber Viton rings were used on the water and oil passages. A Holley 735 cfm carburetor, a mild hydraulic camshaft, an aluminum high-rise intake manifold, aluminum valve covers, free-flowing exhaust manifolds, a dual-point distributor, and a six-quart oil pan were all part of the Boss 429 engine.

The engine was massive for that era. Of course, now such engines are the norm for Mustangs.

Ford installed two versions of this engine, known as the S and T engines, in the Boss 429 Mustang. The S engines had much larger connecting rods, using ½-inch rod bolts (the rods weighed almost three pounds each!), similar to the ones used on the NASCAR 429s, while the more common T engine used slightly stronger production 429 rods. For once, Ford rated the engines accurately: 375 hp at 5200 rpm, as dynamometer tests showed that this was the actual power output of both versions of the street Boss 429 engine.

In spite of all these impressive specifications, the Boss 429 did not turn out to be the street terror it was expected to be. The small carburetor, mild camshaft, and heavy valve train limited performance tremendously. Chrysler's 426 Hemi, on the other hand, was a real tiger, with two four-barrel carburetors and, until 1970, a pretty strong mechanical camshaft.

Still, the Boss 429 could keep up with the 428CJ Mustangs and from 60 mph on, would leave them behind. Its handling was superior to that of any other big-block Mustang and better than most of the smaller-engine Mustangs as well. The revised front suspension geometry, wider track, and rear sway bar combined to eliminate most of the understeer from the chassis. The Boss 429 was more precise, quicker, and more responsive during cornering. It felt more like a detuned racer.

PROSPECTS

The majority of 1969 Boss 429s that have survived are relatively low mileage cars. The reason for this was that the engine was notorious for spinning bearings, because the stock oil capacity was inadequate when the engine was revved over 6000 rpm. Although the usual hot rod engine modifications could transform this engine into the monster racer it was intended to be, any Boss 429 (and Boss 302 as well) has considerably more value restored to stock specifications. As a result many of these cars just got parked early on when their owners found out that they weren't the killer street machines they could have been (and most likely after spinning the bearings, too).

Production exceeded the NASCAR minimum of 500 with 899 units built, but the Boss 429 is still one of the rarest of Mustangs. It is also one of the most difficult to fake.

Boss 429 Mustangs have appreciated well over the years because they are so unique and have so many specially designed features and parts. They are more difficult to restore than other Mustangs but are worth the challenge.

A point worth noting is that the Boss 302 and Boss 429 are the only Mustangs that have the car's consecutive unit number inscribed on the engine. On the Boss 302, this is at the top rear of the block, while on the Boss 429 it is at the rear and side. Obviously, a Boss 429 or 302 with the original engine will be more valuable.

6
1970 Mustang

PRODUCTION

63A 2dr fastback	39,470
65A 2dr hardtop	77,161
76A convertible	6,199
63B 2dr fastback	6,464
65B 2dr hardtop	5,408
76B convertible	1,474
63C fastback Mach 1	40,970
65E 2dr hardtop Grande	13,581
Total	190,727

Specials

428CJ	3,959
Boss 302	7,013
Boss 429	499

Impressive as the Mustang line-up continued to be in 1969, sales lagged behind those in 1968, and 1968 had been considerably less successful than the 1967 model-year sales. Obviously, increased competition in and stabilization (and beginning of the decline) of the pony car market hurt Mustang sales. Still, the Mustang outsold all other pony cars.

The front grille was the biggest change on the 1970 Mustang. The most noticeable were the two 7 inch headlights. This is the Mach 1. Photo courtesy of Jerry Heasley

It's reasonable to wonder why Ford kept building new and better Mustangs while sales were in decline. The answer is that car companies strive to maintain market share and customer loyalty by meeting identified needs. A prospective buyer may be attracted by a Mach 1, but Ford hopes he or she will leave the dealership the proud owner of a Ford product, even if it isn't a Mustang.

In 1970 there was some minor juggling of the options list, plus styling revisions to differentiate the car from the 1969 models. In terms of performance, however, there was plenty for the enthusiast to choose from.

The most obvious styling change was the front grille. Ford reverted to using dual headlights. The lights were located within the grille opening. The tail lights were recessed in a flat rear tail light panel, and the simulated side scoops on the SportsRoof were deleted, as had been done on the 1969 Boss 302, resulting in a cleaner look. The simulated side vent, which had a tacky look to it, was also deleted from the hardtops and convertibles. Overall, the 1970 Mustang looked a little more sedate than did the mean 1969 models.

The Sports Slats, rear wing, and Shaker hood scoop were now available as separate options to enhance the image of even the most humble Mustang. Naturally the slats and wing were only available for the

The most prominent change on the 1970 Mustang was the location of the single 7-inch headlight per side inside the grille. Simulated scoops took the place of the outer headlights.

The 1970 Mustang rear taillight panel was now flat rather than concave and the taillights were recessed.

SportsRoof, while the Shaker could be had in any Mustang body style as long as its engine size was 351 c.i. or larger.

The interior remained essentially the same, but the high-back bucket seats became standard equipment. Only one fancy interior option was available, the Decor Group. It included simulated wood appliqués on the dash and door panels, a deluxe steering wheel, dual color-keyed racing mirrors and rocker panel, and wheel opening moldings. A

The Mach 1 now had aluminum rocker panel moldings with large Mach 1 lettering replacing the previous year's tape stripe. Also on the Mach 1 were these realistic-looking wheel covers.

The 1970 Mach 1 interior. The steering wheel was different from the 1969 version and the ignition key was moved to the steering wheel.

noticeable change was the relocation of the ignition switch to the steering column. This was an industry-wide move designed to deter theft. It's too bad that as a deterrent it didn't really work. Other interior alterations involved detail changes to accommodate such things as different seatbelts.

Ford made some important mechanical changes as well. Mustangs equipped with dual exhausts got a more conventional system with two mufflers, rather than the single transverse muffler used in years before. A rear anti-roll bar was added to the Competition Suspension package to improve handling. This was a bar measuring ½ inch on the 351 Mustangs, while the 428s got a ⅝ inch rear bar. The front bar on the Mach 1s measured ¹⁵⁄₁₆ inch. Another minor change that benefited handling was the switch to seven-inch wide rims on the Mach 1s.

Engine line-up included an addition and a change. The old 390 c.i. was finally retired, but more significantly, a new 351 c.i. joined the options list. This was the 351 Cleveland (351C), that shared the same bore and stroke as the 351W. In reality, it was a completely different engine. The design of the cylinder head made the engine what it was, and the 351C had the best-designed cylinder heads of any Ford factory V-8, short of a Hemi. It is true that Chevrolet pioneered the canted-valve head design, but Ford further refined it.

Unlike the 351W and other small-blocks, the 351C was designed with two separate cylinder heads, known as the two-barrel and four-barrel heads. The more common 2V (two-barrel carburetor) cylinder head had smaller ports and valves (2.04 inches intake, 1.65 inches exhaust) and non-adjustable rocker arms. All 2V heads had an open combustion chamber design for low compression and emission. The 4V (four-barrel carburetor) cylinder heads had much larger ports and valves (2.19 inches intake, 1.71 inches exhaust) and the 1970-71 versions had closed or quench-type combustion chambers. In fact, the 4V heads were very similar to the Boss 302 heads. Besides the larger ports and valves, the 4V heads also came with cylinder blocks that had four-bolt mains.

The 2V heads out-flowed the 351W by a wide margin. The 2V version, with its 9:1 compression ratio and 350 cfm two-barrel carburetor, was rated at 250hp at 4600 rpm. The 4V engine, with a 470 cfm carburetor and 11:1 compression, was rated by Ford at 300hp at 5400 rpm.

The 428s remained unchanged; however, you could now order the Drag Pack option group with the 428CJ-R engine, which effectively transformed the engine to a 428SCJ. As in 1969, it came with a 3.91:1 or 4.30:1 axle ratio, engine oil cooler, and stronger connecting rods. A total of 3,959 Mustangs with the 428CJ were built. 800 of these were non-Ram Air.

Transmission choices remained the same in 1970, although all four-speed manual transmissions included a Hurst shifter and T-handle.

SPECIALS

The only change in the model line-up was the deletion of the GT Equipment Group—no more Mustang GTs (until 1982, that is). The Grande got some changes. The interior got a hound's-tooth pattern on the seats and a half-vinyl roof. A full vinyl roof was optional. There was also the addition of a new plastic rear taillight panel. 13,583 were built.

Here is a 1970 Mach 1 that has the optional Magnum wheels and front spoiler.

The 1970 Mach 1 from the rear.

The Mach 1

The appearance of the Mach 1 did change. The rocker panels were covered with a full-length aluminum cover and had large Mach 1 lettering on the front. The blacked-out hood disappeared; a hood with black or white stripes with engine size numbers around the hood scoop took its place. The simulated hood scoop, painted black, was standard equipment on all Mach Is, but the Shaker, as mentioned earlier, was optional with the 351 engines. The NASCAR-type hood-pins were replaced by twist-type click units. The Mach 1 grille received two sport lamps that enhanced the appearance of the Mach 1 more than anything else. The sport lamps made the 1970 Mach 1 resemble the more aggressive look of the 1969 model. The rear tail light area got a honeycomb design panel, and the tail stripe was enlarged and had much larger Mach 1 lettering.

Other visual changes included mag-style hubcaps mounted on 14x7 inch steel wheels and chrome oval exhaust tips for the four-barrel engines. Black-painted styled steel wheels were a no-cost option. The interior of the Mach I still had wood-grain appliqués on the doors, dash, console, and steering wheel.

The 428CJ Mach was still probably the fastest you could go in the quarter-mile in a street car. Competition, however, was getting stronger. Pontiac came out with a 455 c.i. Trans Am model. And of course, Chrysler, nearly six years after the Mustang was introduced, finally fielded its own true pony cars. The Barracuda and the Challenger with the 440 Six Pack or the 426 Chrysler Hemi were real brutes, but they were a lot heavier than the Mustang. All pony cars were limited by tire technology. Ford chose to put more effort behind its promotional campaign, and sales hit a high of 7,013 units.

Boss 302

The 1970 Boss 302 used the SportsRoof body with the color-keyed mirrors and front spoiler. These cars were shipped to the dealers without having the spoiler installed. It was up to the dealers to install it, and apparently, dealers didn't always do so. As a result, occasionally Boss 302s turn up without the front spoiler.

Exterior color selection expanded with the addition of the bright Grabber color series. The rear deck and tail light area remained blacked-out, but the side C-stripes were eliminated. They were replaced by a hood stripe

The 1970 Boss 302 and the optional Shaker hood scoop.

This is a close-up of the stock Boss 302 trim ring and hubcap combination. The Magnum 500 wheels became optional in 1970.

flanked by two smaller stripes that turned at the fender and went along the sides of the car, incorporating the Boss 302 lettering.

Other visual changes included the 15x7 inch wheels that used an aluminum hubcap and trim ring combination, although the handsome chrome Magnum 500 wheels were optional. Tire size was still F60xI5. In addition, the rear wing, Sports Slats, and the Shaker hood scoop became an option on the Boss 302, and some 302s even had a hood-mounted tachometer. As with other Mustangs, the Boss 302 got the high-back bucket seats as standard equipment, and while most still got the standard interior, the Decor Group was optional.

The engine received some minor modifications that tended to improve performance. Intake valve size was reduced to 2.19 inches from 2.23 inches. Even the 2.19 inch valves were too large for a street engine measuring 302 c.i. For example, the Chevrolet 454 big-block used a 2.19 inch intake valve, and the 302 c.i. Z-28 motor got along with ones measuring just 2.02 inches. The large valves helped engine breathing over 6,500 rpm. Other changes included the substitution of the cross-drilled crankshaft for a unit that was not cross-drilled. Apparently, it made no difference in a street engine and enabled Ford to save a few dollars. The chrome valve covers were replaced by finned aluminum versions, although some early 1970 Boss 302s did have chrome covers. The Boss 302 also got the dual-muffler exhaust system, a ½-inch rear anti-roll bar, a front anti-roll bar of $^{11}/_{16}$ inch, and the Hurst shifter for crisper shifts.

The hood stripes that came on the Boss 302 were also used on the Mach 1.

This is a Boss that doesn't have the rear wing or Sports Slats. It almost looks bare, doesn't it?

Another racing Boss 302 from the 1970 era. This car was driven by George Follmer.

Racing Boss 302s look almost stock. It's quite likely that modern day SVT Cobras would out-accelerate 1970-era Boss 302s.

The year 1970 marked the end of Boss 302 production. The SCCA changed the rules for the 1971 Trans-Am season, allowing engines with a maximum displacement of 350 c.i. This prompted Ford to drop the expensive Boss 302 and replace it with the Boss 351. Ford of Canada did build a few 1971 Boss 302s, although no exact figures are available.

In spite of the fact that significantly more 1970 Boss 302s were built, there doesn't seem to be much of a dollar difference between the two years in terms of collector prices. If you are interested in one, I would suggest you get one that has a rebuilt engine because of the piston problem.

Boss 429

The 1970 Boss 429 remained essentially the same, receiving only minor body and mechanical changes. Production of the Boss 429 declined to 499 units. It should also be noted that all Boss 429 Mustangs were built from January to December 1969, with a short break in the summer to accommodate the model changeover.

The Boss 429 had some changes for 1970. The wheels had a small center cap the hood scoop was painted black.

Aside from the 1970 Mustang body changes, the 1970 Boss 429 can be distinguished by its black hood scoop, regardless of body color. Exterior color choice expanded and included the Grabber colors. The Boss 429 continued to use the chrome Magnum 500 wheels, although these now had a small center hubcap like the Boss 302.

If you look at Mustangs a lot, you'll notice that many Mustangs have a nose-up attitude. Perhaps it's tires or the springs. The only Mustang that came from the factory with a nose-down attitude was the Boss 429. This was the result of lowering the front end suspension by 1 inch.

Only one Boss 429 engine was available, the T series. Some of these were tagged "A," as they had minor modifications to the emission system. The major change was the use of a mechanical lifter camshaft, the same unit found on the 429SCJ wedge engine, which was supposed to increase horsepower by 30hp at 6000 rpm. The engine, however, was still rated at 375hp. The only suspension change was the use of a Boss 302-type rear anti-roll bar measuring ⅝ inch, and mounted over the rear axle.

Inside, the basic Mustang interior was standard equipment, while the Decor Group was optional.

Incidentally, Ford built two Boss 429 Cougars. There were also two Quarter Horse prototypes, which have been located. The Quarter Horse was a 1970 Mustang that used a Shelby nose with the Boss 429 engine, but never reached production. Another Boss 429 variant was a unique mid-engine 1970 Mustang, with the engine mounted behind the rear seat. There is reason to believe that this car exists because it was not sent to the crusher, as was the normal procedure for prototype cars at Ford engineering.

The scoop looks big when you get close to the Boss 429.

The Boss 429 engine. Supposedly the 1970 version ran better because the engine used a mechanical camshaft.

PROSPECTS

The Boss 429s are Mustangs without equal, simply for their extremely large and complex engines. They are probably the most valuable production Mustang as they satisfy all the prerequisites for collectorship: low production, historical significance, and uniqueness.

From an investment angle, all Boss 429s will continue to appreciate at a much faster rate than other Mustangs. Originality is much more important here, since any missing special Boss 429 parts (and there are a lot of special parts) are extremely difficult to replace. Due to their low production numbers, reproduction of replacement parts has remained impractical for most people.

You'll also find many of these cars have the rear wing and Sports Slats, although they weren't originally available as an option from Ford. Although not original in the strictest sense, these items really enhance the car's image. Offering tremendous acceleration and handling to match, the Boss 429 represented the high point in big-block Mustangs and exemplified the extreme to which manufacturers went in their quest for supremacy on the track.

Worth mentioning, too, are the Grabber SportsRoof Mustangs available in 1970. If you wanted to enhance the appearance of a base SportsRoof, you could order your Mustang with the Grabber side stripes. There were two versions: one looked exactly like the 1969 Boss 302 side stripes but without the 302 lettering, and the other looked like a plain stripe, hockey stick. These incorporated either 302 or 351 numerals for engine size. Most of these Mustangs came with the hubcap and trim ring combination.

In 1970 Ford still produced special Mustangs for specific areas of the country. One of the more interesting was the Twister Special made for the Kansas City District. The Twister Special consisted of a group of 96 consecutively produced and numbered Mach 1s, all painted Grabber Orange. The sides of the car got a unique side stripe, while the rear fenders got the Twister decal. Forty-eight of these were equipped with the 428SCJ engine, while the other 48 came with the 351C four-barrel engine.

The 1970 Mustangs, along with the 1969 models, are very popular. There are plenty of choices if you are looking for a performance Mustang. The only exceptions are the rarer Boss 429s and 302s. You'll note that only 3,959 Mustangs came with the 428CJ engine in 1970 (800 of which were non-Ram–Air).

Both the 1969 and 1970 models are better driving cars than their predecessors, and they look a lot

The claim to fame on the 1970 Twister is the side stripes and decals. Photo courtesy of Brad Bowling

The 1970 Twister from the rear. Photo courtesy of Brad Bowling

like the early Mustangs, which is important to many people. Good looks and greater ease of driving should cause these Mustangs to generate considerable activity among collectors.

7
1971–1972 Mustang

PRODUCTION

1971

65D 2dr hardtop	65,696
63D 2dr SportsRoof	23,956
76D convertible	6,121
65F 2dr hardtop Grande	17,406
63R 2dr SportsRoof Mach 1	36,499
Total	149,678

Specials

Boss 351	1,806
429CJ	1,865

1972

65D 2dr hardtop	57,350
63D 2dr SportsRoof	15,622
76C convertible	6,121
65F 2dr hardtop Grande	18,045
63R 2dr SportsRoof Mach 1	27,675
Total	125,093

Specials

351CJ-HO	398

The year 1971 saw the last major restyling of the first-generation Mustang. The Mustang grew in every dimension except height, while maintaining the original's proportions. Wheelbase increased to 109 inches; track grew by 3 inches, length by 2.1 inches, and weight by about 200 pounds. When compared to a 1965 Mustang, the changes were far more obvious. The 1971 was longer, wider, and heavier, by about 800 pounds. The restyling sought to create the illusion that it was larger. From the interior, the hood looked absolutely massive, yet the car was only 0.5 inch longer and slightly narrower than the redesigned 1970 Camaro. The model included a rear seat, air conditioning, and, for the first time, power windows.

Only 1,865 Mach 1s and 18 convertibles had the 429CJ/SCJ engine. The engine compartment was designed from the start to accept the big V-8 but the market had moved away by 1971.

Buyers had the choice of two interior option groups. The Decor Group came with knitted vinyl or cloth seats, door panels with wood appliqués, a deluxe two-spoke steering wheel, dual color-keyed mirrors, and chrome rocker panels and wheel well moldings. The Mach 1 Sports Interior was also available as an option on any SportsRoof Mustang. It included a different upholstery on the seats, the deluxe steering wheel and door panels, the instrument group, an electric clock, and a special carpet with integral rubber floor mats.

The base engine was the 250 c.i. six-cylinder rated at 145hp. Two transmissions were available—either a three-speed manual or a three-speed automatic. This was followed by 210hp 302 two-barrel carburetor, 240hp 351C two-barrel carburetor, 285hp 351C four-barrel carburetor, and two

The rear of the 1971 Mustang was almost flat and was probably the reason that the Sport Slats were not available as an option.

The standard interior of a 1971–72 Mustang.

The basic transportation 302 c.i. on a
1971–72 Mustang.

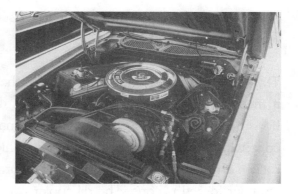

The 351-CJ had a lot more spunk.

429s rated at 370hp and 375hp respectively. Only the four-barrel 351C and 429s came with the four-speed manual as standard; the automatic was optional.

Late in the model year, another 351C engine was released. This was the 351CJ rated at 280hp, with a lower compression ratio of 8.6:1.

The most interesting engine in 1971 was the 429. The 429 c.i., a destroked version of the 460 c.i. that powered Lincolns, made its first appearance in a 1968 Thunderbird. This was Ford's answer to the big-block Chevrolet engine, and it was similar in design, but featured a refined cylinder head port configuration. The 429 c.i. was also designed to be a cleaner engine, producing fewer emissions than the FE series engines it replaced. When the 429/460 was designed, Ford was also preparing for a future that never materialized. There had been plans, for example, for a 501 c.i. version, initially for use in the big luxury cars.

The big 429SCJ is in this 1971 Mach 1.

Mustangs could be had with three versions of the 429: the 429CJ, the 429CJ-R (Ram-Air) and the 429SCJ-R. All of them used large intake and exhaust valves (2.25 inches and 1.72 inches respectively), and had an 11.3:1 compression ratio and the large-port cylinder heads. Like the 351C, the 429 c.i. was available with two sets of cylinder heads. The small-port, small-valved heads were used in nonperformance applications and were not ever installed in a Mustang. The 429CJ and 429CJ-R were rated at 370hp at 5400 rpm. They used a hydraulic cam, and some early versions had adjustable rocker arms. More importantly, the engine came with four-bolt main caps for increased durability. In an unusual move, both the 429CJ and 429CJ-R came with a Rochester Quadrajet carburetor, flowing 700 cfm.

The most powerful engine available was the 429SCJ-R. Available only with the Drag Pack option, it meant either a 3.91:1 Traction Lok or 4.11:1 Detroit Locker rear, and was rated at only five horsepower more than the 429CJ. Internally, the 429SCJ-R was modified and strengthened to cope with the extra power it produced. A higher performance mechanical camshaft with adjustable rocker arms and a Holley 780 cfm carburetor replaced the Quadrajet. The 429SCJ-R also used stronger forged pistons. The oil cooler was not part of the Drag Pack option, although some cars have turned up that have it.

The 429s were available with either a close-ratio four-speed transmission or the C-6 automatic. Power steering and power brakes were mandatory with these heavyweights. Speaking of power steering, Mustangs with the optional Competition Suspension used a variable-ratio steering box made by GM.

Only 1,255 Mustangs were built with the 429CJ and 429CJ-R engines, and even fewer with the 429SCJ-R: 610 cars.

SPECIALS

The Grande was again available in 1971, catering to those interested in a luxury hardtop. The Grande had a standard vinyl roof, and a gussied-up interior that included the deluxe two-spoke steering wheel and instrument panel appliqués, rocker panel and wheel well opening moldings, color-keyed mirrors, and appropriate Grande identification.

Mach 1

The high-performance Mustang was the Mach 1. The package included color-keyed rearview mirrors, a unique honeycomb front grille with integral Sportlamps, a color-keyed bumper unique to the Mach 1, a redesigned gas cap, Mach 1 fender decals, a Mach 1 rear deck lid stripe, a honeycomb tail light panel, and black- or Argent-painted lower body areas depending on the exterior color. The front and rear valence panels were similarly painted. The four-barrel 351s and all 429s came with dual exhaust extensions. The NASA hood was a no-cost option on the Mach 1 with the basic engine, and standard equipment on all other engines. Having the NASA hood did not mean that

A 1971 Mustang. It still had the usual Mustang styling cues, but they were being rapidly lost in all that sheet-metal.

This is a 1971 Mach 1.

the Mustang was equipped with Ram-Air. Hoods with functional Ram-Air came with Ram-Air decals on either side of the scoops.

Unlike in previous Mach 1s, the standard interior was the basic Mustang interior. The fancier Mach I Sports Interior was optional. The standard Mach 1 wheels were the brushed aluminum trim rings and hubcaps sporting whitewall E70x14 tires with the 302 and 351C cars, while the 429s came with RWL F70xl4 tires. A more desirable option was the 15x7 Chrome Magnum 500 wheels with Goodyear F60x15 RWL tires. All Mach 1s came with the Competition Suspension, which had the usual heavier-duty springs and shocks and 7/8 inch front and 1/2 inch rear anti-roll bars. The 429CJ Mach 1s (and other Mustangs powered by this engine) came with a larger 5/8 inch rear anti-roll bar.

The base engine on the Mach 1 was the 302 c.i.; this really wasn't enough engine for a Mustang that was evoking such a racer image. The two-barrel carburetor 351C was next on the options list, but for passable street performance, the 285hp four-barrel 351C was necessary.

The only way to identify a 429-powered Mach 1 was by the hood decals. With the 429CJ, straight-line performance was more than acceptable, being mid- to high 13 seconds in the quarter-mile. Much like other big-block Mustangs, handling was not good when pushed hard.

A nice set of modern radial tires will make a tremendous difference, provided you aren't into strict originality, as will some minor suspension tuning.

Boss 351

The last Boss Mustang to be built was the Boss 351, and it too, lived up to the Boss concept of a car that could accelerate, brake, and handle with the best that Detroit could offer. In stock form, the Boss 351 equaled or surpassed the acceleration of other big-block Mustangs (and other pony cars),

The other hot Mustang in 1971 was the Boss 351. It took the place of the Boss 302 and 429. It looked a lot like the Mach 1, and had a chrome front bumper.

and its weight distribution provided better handling and braking. Like its predecessors, the Boss 351 was a complete package, with few options.

The Boss 351 used the Mach 1 SportsRoof, with some differences. The functional NASA hood was standard equipment, but the Boss 351 used a chrome front bumper rather than the color-keyed bumper of the Mach 1. The hood, rocker panels, and front and rear valence panels were black or argent to contrast with the exterior paint color, and all Boss 351s had a front spoiler.

The Boss 351 used the standard Mustang interior, but the three-pod instrument package was standard equipment. Other interiors were optional.

The Boss 351 had a unique side stripe and small Boss 351 decals on the fenders and rear deck lid. Later in the model year, however, the Mach 1 could be optioned with these stripes as well, diluting the impact of the Boss 351.

Boss 351 decals were used on the front fenders. These are the standard trim ring and hub cap wheels; the chrome Magnum 500 wheels were optional.

Other standard items were the 15x7 brushed aluminum wheels with the Goodyear F60x15 tires, but the 15x7 chrome Magnum 500 wheels were optional. The rear wing spoiler was optional, but no rear window slats were available from Ford, probably due to the almost flat angle of the rear window.

All Boss 351s came with a wide-ratio four-speed manual transmission that used a Hurst Shifter, a 3.91:1 rear axle ratio, and the Competition Suspension with the larger 5/8 inch rear anti-roll bar.

As with other Boss Mustangs, the heart of the Boss package was the engine. The Boss 351 was Ford's most advanced medium block engine. Like the four-barrel 351C in the 1970 Mach 1, the Boss 351 used a four-bolt main block and the large-port, big-valve cylinder heads. Due to the mechanical lifter camshaft, however, the Boss 351 used adjustable rocker arms. The engine was also equipped with specially treated forged steel rods, and the crankshaft was specially chosen for high nodularity. The Boss 351 came with an aluminum intake manifold, but unlike previous Boss engines, it used a 750 cfm Motorcraft carburetor. Compression ratio was a high 11:1. Ford rated this 351C just like the Boss 302, at 330hp at 5400 rpm. Considering the high-13- to low-14-second quarter-mile times and the weight of the car (3,750 lbs), Ford was obviously underrating the output of this engine.

Overall, the Boss 351 handled better than the Mach 1s because it had large tires and a slightly bigger rear anti-roll bar. It could out-accelerate other cars with much bigger engines and had much better low-end response than did previous Boss Mustangs.

The Boss 351 engine was just as good as the Boss 302 and 429 on the street. It used a mechanical lifter camshaft.

Only 1,806 Boss 351 Mustangs were built. These trail other Bosses in value because of the larger 1971 body style, but they are still a worthwhile investment.

Later in the model year, Ford further diluted the performance image of the Mach 1 and Boss 351 by offering features from both cars on the hardtop. The Sports hardtop used the Mach 1 grille, NASA hood, color-keyed front bumper, Boss 351 side stripes, lower body paint, and color-keyed mirrors. It may have helped hardtop sales, but Ford was using these features to promote sales and thus diluting their "cool" factor.

1972

The 1972 Mustangs stand out simply because they don't stand out. Differences between a 1971 and a 1972 are hard to spot. For the first time, the Mustang's basic styling went unchanged as Ford concentrated more on meeting emissions and safety regulations. Also, development of the Mustang II was well along the way.

Although the Mustang looked the same, some changes were made, particularly under the hood. The Boss 351 model was dropped, as were the big-block 429s. The top engine was the 351CJ, which was introduced in late 1971. Rated at 266hp, using the SAE net rating, it was a respectable engine, even though the compression ratio was dropped to 8.8:1. It was still equipped with the better 351C 4V carburetor heads.

Next in line was the two-barrel 351C rated at 177hp, while the two-barrel 302 managed to pump out 140hp. The standard engine, the 250 c.i. six-cylinder, put out 98hp.

This is a rare 1972 Mach 1 with the 351-HO engine. It was Ford's last attempt to build a performance engine. Only 366 were installed in SportsRoof models.

The 1972 Mach 1 with a 351-HO engine.

Ford made one last gasp at performance briefly during the beginning of the model year, however. This was with the limited 351CJ-HO (for High Output), available with any Mustang body. Basically, the 351CJ-HO was a detuned version of the 1971 Boss 351 engine. It was rated at 275hp at 6000 rpm. All the good pieces of the Boss 351 were included, but the compression ratio was reduced to 8.8:1 so that the engine could run on regular gas.

Mandatory options with the 351CJ-HO were power front disc brakes, Competition Suspension, wide-ratio four-speed manual transmission, a 3.91:1 Traction Lok rear axle, and F60x15 RWL Goodyear tires on 15x7 wheels. Incidentally, any 1972 Mustang that came with the Magnum 500 wheels also had to have the Competition Suspension, as it was a mandatory option. Quarter-mile

The decal on the air cleaner lid is an obvious giveaway. Otherwise, the car ran pretty much like the Boss 351 did.

All 351-HO engines were equipped with a rev limited mounted on the right shock tower.

times were recorded at 15.1 seconds at 95.6 mph and 0-60 mph at 6.6 seconds, by Car and Driver magazine.

There were 19 hardtops, 366 SportRoofs and 13 convertibles equipped this way, making them the last true performance Mustangs of the first generation.

Noteworthy changes on the 1972 were as follows: The Exterior Decor Group, available on hardtops and convertibles, consisted of the Mach 1 grille and Sportlamps, color keyed front bumpers, lower body

Ford further diluted the performance image of the Mach 1 and Boss 351 by offering features from both cars on the hardtop. This was the Sports Hardtop.

paint treatment, special moldings, and brushed aluminum trim rings and hubcaps. You could also get the Mach 1 tape stripes on convertibles. The NASA hood was still available, but the Ram-Air option was limited to the 351C two-barrel carburetor engine during the second half of the model year.

The Sprint package was available on the 1972 Mustang convertible and SportsRoof. What made it stand out was its white paint and dual blue and red hood stripes, as well as the blue and red lower and rear body treatment.

The Mach 1 was unchanged from 1971, although the rear pop-open gas cap was replaced by the regular production cap. The Grande, too, was unchanged, with the exception of different side stripes.

Only one new model was introduced in 1972, the Sprint. The Sprint featured a special exterior paint treatment to coordinate with a unique interior. It was not a performance package by any means and was available on hardtops and fastbacks. All Sprints were painted white with red and blue stripes on the hood, rear panel, and lower body area. A USA shield decal was placed on the rear quarter panel—patriotic indeed. All Sprints came with the Exterior Decor Group, dual color-keyed mirrors, and E70x14 whitewall tires on wheels with brushed aluminum trim rings and hubcaps. This Sprint combination was known as Sprint Package A. Package B replaced the 14-inch wheels with the 15x7 chrome Magnum 500s, using the F60x15 RWL Goodyear tires.

There was, however, a special run of 50 Sprint convertibles made for Washington, D.C. These were used in the Cherry Day Parade, and each car represented one state.

A USA shield was used in the rear fender.

Sprint Package B was identical to Sprint Package A, except for chrome Magnum 500 wheels and Competition Suspension.

Sprint Package B from the rear.

Here is a close-up of the Sprint A hood paint treatment.

PROSPECTS

Obviously, the most collectible 1971s are the Boss 351s and the 429-powered Mach 1s. However, convertibles, as in previous model years, are also highly collectible, and the more options, the better. As with earlier Mustangs, rust is a problem, but the availability of reproduction body panels is limited. The same applies for most of the interior trim and upholstery. It is much more of a challenge to restore the 1971–73 Mustangs.

It is true that the 1971–73 Mustangs may be the least popular of the first generation Mustangs, but they do have a solid core of support. One of these can also be a good alternative to some of the pricier early Mustangs.

Of all the 1972 Mustangs, the 351CJ HO Mustangs hold some special significance because they are the last true high-performance Mustangs of the first generation. If you are interested in one, be prepared to pay because they are quite rare.

In 1972, sales for the Mustang continued to slide, reflecting the downward trend in the pony car market. Still, the Mustang ran number one, ahead of all other pony cars.

8
1973 Mustang

PRODUCTION

63D 2dr SportsRoof	10,820
65D 2dr hardtop	51,480
76D convertible	11,853
65F 2dr hardtop Grande	25,274
63R 2dr SportsRoof Mach 1	35,440
Total	134,867

The last year for the big-bodied Mustang was 1973. Although restyled slightly, it differed little from the 1972 model. The Mustang had grown too big and alienated many in its customer base. Cars like the Maverick, Chevy Nova, and Plymouth Duster were selling well, and in many ways they were closer to the original Mustang, at least in terms of size. Part of the original's allure had been its size, as it was trim and compact. The later Mustang was on its way to becoming an intermediate sedan. The Cougar, by 1973, had already graduated to intermediate size, giving up all pretense of being a pony car.

In fact, while Ford's German-built Capri was enjoying modest success, the car that captured the hearts of many enthusiasts was the Datsun 240Z. Ford would try to bring back those who left with the 1974 Mustang II, but in the meantime there was still the 1973 Mustang.

The 1973 Mach 1 continued in 1973 with minor changes. Photo courtesy of Brad Bowling

The 1973 Mach 1 from the rear. Photo courtesy of Brad Bowling

The 351CJ had made it clear that performance was no longer what mattered. The 1965 Mustang with the 271hp 289 c.i. was capable of out-accelerating the last big Mustang. At least these 1973 Mustangs had the potential for decent performance, if the usual hop-up techniques were employed.

The most noticeable change on the 1973 Mustang was its front grille and 5-mph bumper.

The most noticeable exterior change was the new grille, which used vertical parking lights at each end. All 1973 Mustangs used a color-keyed front bumper designed to pass the new (for 1973) 5 mph crash test. Considering that most 1973 cars sported big battering rams for bumpers, Ford did a nice job on the Mustang. Rear bumper standards weren't quite so strict yet, but the chrome rear bumper was mounted a little bit further from the body than the 1972's bumper had been.

The Decor Group was still available. A honeycomb grille with a small Mustang emblem took the place of the standard egg-crate grille. The headlight bezels were also blacked out, not the chrome of the standard Mustangs. Ford also used this grille on the Mach 1. The lower body side paint treatment and the brushed aluminum trim ring and hubcap combination rounded out the package.

The wheels on this Grande were the same as those used on the 1970 model.

The side tape stripe, a Boss 351 original, was still an option available in conjunction with the Decor Group. This allowed even the nonperformance Mustangs to look

A 1973 Mustang Mach 1.

The interior of the 1973 Grande. It had most of the luxury items available.

The basic engine—the 302 c.i. with a two-barrel carburetor rated at 141hp.

hot. The Mach 1 Sports Interior was still available, as was the rear wing and almost all of the 1972 options. Noticeably absent were the 15x7 Magnum 500 wheels. 14-inch forged aluminum wheels took their place on the options list.

The Mach 1 and Grande were, again, relatively unchanged. The Mach 1 did get a new side stripe that began at the front fender and ended just before the rear wheel well. Engine and drivetrain combinations were unchanged. The 351CJ was the top engine option but was not available with Ram-Air. Only the two-barrel version of the 351 could be had with Ram-Air, at extra cost of course.

Some mechanical improvements did appear, in spite of 1973's being the last year for the first-generation Mustang. Suspension travel was increased by a negligible ¼ inch.

PROSPECTS

You'll find that 1973 Mustangs fetch slightly more than a comparable 1971 or 1972 model (excluding the 1971 429s and Boss 351). This higher price reflects the cars' status as the last of the breed. The Mustang had strayed too far from its origins as a powerful street racer and became just another car, losing the broad appeal it once had.

9
1965–2007
Shelby Mustangs

PRODUCTION

1965

GT350 street prototype	1
GT350 street cars	521
1966 prototype	1
Drag cars	4
Competition prototype	2
Competition production cars	34
Total	562

1966

1966 GT350 prototype	2
Standard GT350	1,365
Paxton prototype	1
Hertz GT350H prototype	2
Hertz GT350H	999
Drag cars	4
GT350 convertibles	4
Total	2,378

1967

GT350   1,175
GT500 2,048
GT500 notchback prototype 1
GT500 convertible prototype 1

Total   3,225

1968

GT500 notchback prototype	1
GT350 fastbacks	803
GT350 fastback Hertz cars	224
GT350 convertibles	404
GT500 fastbacks	1,044
GT500 fastback Hertz cars	2
GT500 convertibles	402
GT500KR fastbacks	1,053
GT500KR convertibles	517
GT500KR convertibles Hertz cars	1
Total	4,451

1969–70

Barrier test and prototype pilot cars	3
1969 Shelby models	2,361
1970 Shelby models	789
Total 1969–70 production	3,153
Barrier test and prototype pilot cars	3
GT350 fastbacks	935
GT350 fastback Hertz cars	152
GT350 convertibles	194
GT500 fastbacks	1,534
GT500 convertibles	335
Total	3,153
Grand total	**13,769**

Twenty-two years ago, I wrote that there were no more inexpensive Shelby Mustangs left for sale. This has continued to be the case. The Shelby has led the way in appreciation, of all the Mustangs. They have remained the premier Mustang image car. Perhaps the later 1967–70 Mustangs lacked the raw macho appeal of the 1965–66 GT350s, but they have proven themselves easier to live with, and faster when equipped with the big 428 c.i. They also became much better looking.

All 1965 Shelby GT350s were painted white.

The uniqueness and rarity of these cars was recognized from the start by Shelby owners, and they honored the car by forming the Shelby American Automobile Club (SAAC). The club's efforts have resulted in growing recognition, preservation, and appreciation of these classics. Under their care, the Shelby has increased in value, and their consistent and well-organized support has been a boon to Shelby owners and restorers. Although there are other clubs, SAAC has offered the most for the Shelby enthusiasts.

The Shelby Mustangs have always been more than just restyled Mustangs. Even though recent offerings deliver excellent performance, they just don't match the excitement, looks, and presence generated by the original Shelby. They have remained popular because they capture the imagination visually, and back that vision with superior performance.

Shelby Mustangs can safely be expected to continue to set the standard for excellence, and as a group, they are the best Mustang investment available.

1965 SHELBY MUSTANG GT350

Shelbys are all based on the Mustang fastback body style.

The mystique generated by the first generation Shelbys of 1965–1966 has resulted in a lingering and enviable reputation for being the fastest, most powerful, and most performance-oriented of all Mustangs. The feeling has been that they were designed specifically for the enthusiast, with the sole purpose of providing lots of performance. They were just finicky and temperamental enough to make them interesting.

The Shelby interior. Note the competition seat belts.

Definitely not for everybody, the Shelby was as close to a street-level race car as was possible. They were fast, handled beautifully, and looked magnificent.

The story was that Carroll Shelby, who had been extremely successful with the Cobra roadster, agreed in 1964 to partner with Ford. Ford was eager to improve its image as a performance, youth-oriented automaker, and needed a car to compete with GM's Corvette in road racing. The Shelby Mustang did both: It improved Ford's image, and won its class in SCCA's national road race championships from 1965 to 1967. It also achieved numerous other race victories. Even after all this time, original Shelby Mustangs have been successfully raced.

Ford shipped the partially completed 1965 Mustang fastbacks, only in Wimbledon White, to Shelby's plant in Los Angeles to be finished off. The cars did not have rear seats, hoods, or exhaust systems. They did have an engine: the High Performance 289 c.i. 271hp unit. It was mated to an aluminum Borg Warner four-speed manual transmission with a 3.89:1 rear axle ratio. The fastbacks were then re-engineered and modified to Shelby's specifications.

The appearance of the car was then altered to distinguish it from regular production Mustangs. All Mustang identification and emblems were removed, save for the Mustang emblem on the front grille. The grille was changed, and the emblem was moved to the far left. A fiberglass hood with functional scoop took the place of the stock steel hood. A side stripe painted on the lower rocker panel had the GT350 nomenclature at the front. The familiar body stripes, beginning at the front valance panel and ending at the rear one, were optional and were sometimes installed by the Ford dealer. The suspension was modified to greatly improve handling. In fact, the suspension of the street GT350 was identical to the full race version, the only difference being alignment specifications.

A hefty, one-inch front anti-roll bar took the place of the stock part; special pitman and idler arms for improved steering response were installed, as were the highly regarded Koni adjustable shock absorbers. Most importantly, the upper control arm suspension mounting points were lowered for better suspension geometry. In the engine compartment, a stronger brace from the firewall to shock tower (known as the Export Brace) and a Monte Carlo bar added the necessary rigidity to the Mustang's structure. In the rear, over-the-axle traction bars (to combat wheel hop during hard acceleration) and special rebound cables were attached to the axle housing. The brakes were modified as

Some of the early Shelby Mustangs were equipped with these silver painted wheels.

The trunk mounted battery that was standard on the first 300 or so Shelby Mustangs.

well. Manual front disc brakes and large 10x2½ inch rear drums with sintered metallic linings provided stopping power. The springs were also much stiffer.

The 271hp 289 c.i. engine, already a good performer, got a thorough going-over. An aluminum high-rise intake manifold and 715 cfm Holley carburetor replaced the stock cast-iron manifold and Autolite carburetor. Steel Tri-Y design exhaust headers replaced the restrictive exhaust manifolds. The rest of the exhaust system consisted of straight-through mufflers with tailpipes exiting in front of the rear tires—very loud! A special cast-aluminum Cobra oil pan and Cobra valve covers improved engine appearance. The 289 c.i. engine was rated at 306hp at 6000 rpm, but you could easily rev it to 7000 rpm.

Other modifications included a driveshaft safety loop and Detroit Locker differential. To further improve weight distribution, the battery was relocated to the trunk, but this modification was discontinued after the first 300 or so cars.

The standard Mustang black interior was modified with a special dash pod that housed two additional gauges, an 8000 rpm tachometer and an oil pressure gauge. Three-inch competition seatbelts kept the driver in place, and three types of genuine wood steering wheels replaced the stock plastic steering wheel. Early cars came with 15 inch diameter wheels with slotted wheels; later cars came with 15 inch wheels with either slotted spokes or three holes in each spoke. The 1965 Shelby Mustang did not have a rear seat. In its place a fiberglass rear deck shelf was installed that also housed the spare tire.

Painted-on rocker panel stripes in Guardsman Blue (code F) had the GT350 logo. Plain, silver-painted 15x5.5 inch steel wheels (later cars had 15x6 inch rims) with chrome lug nuts were used

The Cragar mags are evident on this Shelby.

This is another R model Shelby. Note the modified rear window.

with 7.75x15 Goodyear Blue Dot tires. Optional, and more attractive, were the Cragar 15x6 inch mags. The full race version of the GT350 was known as the R model. The engine was modified further to increase horsepower to 350hp.

R model Shelby Mustangs had various engine configurations, depending on the track.

The nose of the car differed with the installation of a front apron that improved radiator and brake airflow. The car was made lighter with the use of Plexiglas rear and side windows. Other race-only options included a larger 32 gallon gas tank, additional instrumentation, special racing seats, fireproof interior trim, and a rear side scoop with brake cooling ducts. Wheels were 15x7 inch American Racing mags. All these, plus a few other additions, cost $1,500 over the street GT350—a good deal indeed.

Visually the R model was similar to the street GT350. The result was strong product identification by the buyers, exactly what Ford had intended. Only 34 R models were produced, making them some of the rarest Shelby Mustangs.

Performance for the street GT350 was exemplary. Weighing 2,800 pounds or so, it ran 0–60 mph times in about 6.5 seconds, and quarter-mile times in the high-14

This R model has dual Holley carburetors.

second range. The car handled like a racer, but it was not an easy car to drive. The loud exhaust system, hard brake and clutch pedal pressure, extremely stiff suspension, and lack of power steering limited its appeal to the diehard enthusiast. Accordingly, only 562 Shelby Mustangs, including the 34 R models, were sold in 1965.

1966 SHELBY MUSTANG GT350

The year 1966 was a harbinger of the Shelby Mustang's coming fate. Ford felt that the Shelby Mustangs should try to pay their way, and moved the car away from its original concept in the belief that this would increase sales. By 1969, it had become a styling test-bed for Ford.

However, the 1966 Shelby was not really all that different from the 1965. It was toned down a bit, but was still as fast as the 1965 model. With the addition of the optional Paxton Supercharger, it had even better acceleration. Visually, only minor changes differentiated it. A side scoop was added to duct air to the rear brakes, and side quarter windows in place of the stock extractor vents enhanced the sleekness of the car. In addition, the 1966 Shelby could be had in colors other than white, such as red, blue, green, and black.

The loud side exhaust system was replaced by a conventional system that exited behind the axle and used two conventional mufflers. The Detroit Locker differential and wooden steering wheel became options. The Koni shocks were billed as options, but were the norm.

The first 252 1966 GT350s were actually leftover 1965s updated to 1966 specifications. These retained the important A-arm suspension modification, while the rest of the 1966 Shelbys did not.

Shown here is the Essex Wire R Model Shelby. Only 34 R models were made.

The standard Shelby engine pumped out 306hp.

As a cost-savings measure, the over-the-axle traction bars were replaced by those made by Traction Master Company. The new traction bars fit underneath the springs. They were mounted on cars numbered 800 and above.

In all other areas, however, it was still a true Shelby. The improved brakes and suspension and the powerful 306hp 289 went unchanged. To further increase the GT350's appeal, the C-4 automatic three-speed transmission became optional. The Paxton supercharger also became an option. There were 11 cars outfitted in this manner.

1966 Shelby Mustangs are still raced today. This one is at Lime Rock, CT.

The interior also became more hospitable. The 1966 Shelby Mustangs were equipped with rear seats (some had the fold-down seats), but another cost-cutting measure was the deletion of the wood steering wheel. It was replaced by a plastic woodgrain version, though the wood wheel was still available as an option. The Shelby also got the five-pod Mustang dash instrument cluster. The leftover 1965 cars came with the 15 inch Cragar mags or the 15 inch painted steel wheels. The rest of the 1966s got 14x6 inch gray painted Magnum 500 steel wheels (the Hertz cars came with chrome versions), with 6.95x14 Goodyear Blue Streak tires. However, some cars came with silver painted wheels. Optional were the 14x6½ inch ten-spoke Shelby alloy wheels.

Four GT350 convertibles were made, but these were not originally available to the public. Two were four-speed manual transmission cars (yellow and red) and the other two were automatic transmission equipped cars (green and blue). All convertibles were equipped with air conditioning, automatic transmission, the wood steering wheel, and the ten-spoke Shelby wheels. These four are the rarest of all Shelby Mustangs.

Styling changes for the 1966 Shelby were few. A side scoop was added to duct air to the rear brakes, and side quarter windows in place of the stock extractor vents enhanced the sleekness of the car.

Performance and handling of the 1966 Shelbys remained the same. The changes that were made did not detract from the car. It was still a difficult car to drive, as close to a race car as possible, with performance its sole purpose for being. It was a more civilized performance machine, and so sales reached 2,377 units, including the four convertibles.

The interior was largely a basic Mustang one, with its five pod dash.

Unlike the 1965, the 1966 Shelby was equipped with a fold down rear seat.

1966 SHELBY MUSTANG GT350H

As a promotional ploy, Hertz Rent-A-Car bought 999 Shelby Mustangs for use as rental cars. Most were painted black with gold stripes, but other colors included Candy Apple Red, Sapphire Blue, and Ivy Green. These were slightly different from the regular production Shelby Mustangs. They used chrome Magnum 500 14x6 inch steel wheels, and the automatic transmission cars had a 600 cfm Autolite carburetor rather than the 715 cfm Holley. Most Hertz cars were automatics. All Hertz cars received the GT350H designation.

Hertz claimed to have lost money on the venture, but more than made up for it with the youthful performance image the Shelby provided. In fact, Hertz chose to rent out Shelby Mustangs again in 1968–69, although these cars did not receive the GT350H designation.

Shelby Mustangs became more popular in 1966 with the sale of 999 cars to Hertz, the rental company. Most were painted black with gold striping.

Here are two 1966 Shelby rental cars. The one on the left is black while the other is red.

95

The 1965-66 Shelby Mustangs are considered to be the purest in concept. They delivered uncompromising performance, with comfort and economy being secondary. Ford, with successive models, was able to further tone down the car, increasing its appeal without hurting sales.

1967 SHELBY MUSTANG GT350 AND GT500

The 1967 Shelby was extensively restyled. The nose of the car was extended, and two side scoops took the place of the stock air extractors, while the side brake scoops were carried over from 1966.

When the 1967 Mustang got its first major body restyle, the Shelby Mustang did too. The Shelby Mustang was extensively restyled, based on the fastback body style, to set it off further from the regular production Mustangs. The 1965–66 Shelby was easily identifiable as a Mustang; the 1967 less so.

The nose of the car was extended via the liberal use of fiberglass components, to create a more pointed, meaner look. In many ways, the 1967 Shelby was the forerunner of later production Mustangs. A fiberglass hood, incorporating a large functional hood scoop, took the place of the stock steel hood. Two side scoops took the place of the stock air extractors, while the side brake scoops were carried over from 1966. The rear deck lid formed a ducktail spoiler and the revised tail light panel housed 1967 Cougar tail lights. The large hood-to-tail stripes were eliminated from the Shelby styling package but, again some cars had these stripes applied by the dealer.

Headlight configuration differed from production Mustangs. Two outer low-beam headlights were used in conjunction with two high-beam units mounted within the grille opening. Most of these were mounted in the center, but to comply with certain states' headlight laws, some cars had the lights mounted at each end of the grille opening.

The rear deck lid formed a ducktail spoiler. It really was a sharp-looking car.

This Shelby had plain 15x6 inch stock steel wheels with hubcaps that became a rarity. You just don't see many Shelbys with these hubcaps. Most 1967 cars have either the optional 15x7 inch Kelsey-Hayes Mag Star wheels or the 15x7 inch Shelby mags that became available later in the model year. The tires

The side scoops on the Shelby are reminiscent of the Ford GT40 race cars.

No doubt about it, the Shelby was a mean looking car.

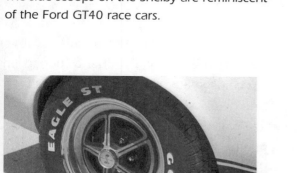

These optional wheels were from Kelsey Hayes.

This 1967 Shelby had lights mounted at each end of the grille opening to comply with a particular state's laws. In this configuration, Shelby styling foreshadowed the 1968 Shelby and the 1969 Mach 1. Photo courtesy of Jerry Heasley

The first 200 or so 1967 Shelby Mustangs came with these lights in the upper side scoop.

The standard 1967 Shelby interior.

were E70x15 Goodyears. Most factory 1967 photos showed the Shelby with hubcaps, which were standard.

The familiar rocker panel stripes with either the GT350 or GT500 designation were standard equipment. Exterior color selection expanded, and the interior could now be ordered in parchment or black. Two additional gauges (amps and oil pressure) were mounted under the dash, but more importantly, each Shelby Mustang got an integral 2-point roll bar (some of the early cars had a 4-point) and an inertia-reel shoulder harness, the first for the American car industry. Beginning in 1967, all Shelbys had 140 mph speedometers and 8000 rpm tachometers.

The K engine was fitted to the 1967 Shelby. It was not available with air conditioning.

The GT350 engine compartment remained the same. The 306hp 289 was available with either a four-speed manual or a three-speed automatic. The Paxton supercharger remained as a special-order option that provided almost big-block acceleration. A total of 28 cars were so equipped.

One big change was the addition of the 428 c.i. engine to the GT500 Shelby designation. Externally, it was similar to the 427 c.i. race engine, but the 428 c.i. had a different bore and stroke (4.13x3.98) for excellent, torquey low-end response. Three of the Medium Riser 427s were installed at the factory. The port and valve sizes were identical to the regular 390 c.i. cylinder heads. The pistons and crank were cast, but the rods were forged steel. Hydraulic lifters

The GT500 engine used two Holley carburetors; with the air cleaner removed, the backwards configuration becomes evident.

The Shelby-modified GT500 engine with its unique oval air cleaner.

were used, but the main difference from other production 428s was the special induction system. A dual-plane aluminum intake manifold used two Holley 600 cfm carburetors. These were mounted backwards and used a unique throttle linkage. All normal driving was done with the front carburetors' two primary barrels. The other six barrels would only be engaged under full throttle acceleration, and this helped mileage quite a bit. The 428 c.i. was also fitted with Cobra valve covers and the Cobra air cleaner. It was rated at 355hp at 5800 rpm.

The big 428 c.i. is the 1967 Shelby Mustang.

Suspension was strictly production Mustang, with heavier springs and shocks. The GT500 used a 15/16 inch front anti-roll bar. Brakes were also production items, with discs in the front and drums in the rear using regular linings. Air conditioning being available as an option that further transformed the Shelby.

The GT350 retained much of the flavor of the earlier GT350s. The lively, responsive 289 had to cope with about 350 pounds more weight, so acceleration times were slower. Handling was better than with regular production Mustangs, as the fiberglass hood helped front-to-rear weight distribution from fifty-three to forty-seven percent.

This is the emblem used on the GT350. It was placed above the GT350 stripe.

This is the GT500 emblem on the rear spoiler.

This GT350 has two stripes plus the optional Shelby wheels.

The GT500 handled pretty much like its cousin, the 390 GT Mustang. Both engines weighed the same in stock form, but the GT500's aluminum intake manifold and fiberglass hood took some of the weight off the front wheels. The GT500's forte was effortless acceleration with quarter-mile times in the low-14-second range, depending on axle ratio and the driver of the car.

Although the Shelby bristled with visual performance cues such as scoops, spoilers, and big wheels and tires, it was no longer the Shelby Mustang that Carroll Shelby had envisioned. It was much more of a compromise, and because of this sales hit 3,225 units for both models. The car was meant to retain the image and excitement of the original GT350 and at the same time appeal to a larger market segment. You could drive it everyday. It was by far the best Mustang available in 1967.

1968 SHELBY MUSTANG GT350, GT500, AND GT500KR

The Shelby line expanded in 1968, with the addition of an impressive convertible. Available with either a small-block or big-block, it accounted for about thirty percent of sales.

We all have a story of a car that we should have kept rather than sold. Mine was a 1968 GT350 convertible. Who would have thought, even in 1976, that these convertibles would become so desirable? Ouch!

In 1968, Ford took complete control of the Shelby operation, and production of these cars was shifted

The 1968 Shelby looked like this. The majority of the changes made were to the nose of the car. The car was actually similar to the 1967 Shelby but with a cleaner look.

to the A. O. Smith facility in Illinois. The nose of the Shelby was restyled again; in fact, Ford made much of this design, as the 1969 regular production Mustangs shared more than a passing resemblance. In 2003 Ford once again styled a concept Mustang that borrowed from the 1968 Shelby. And of course, the 2007 Shelby GT500 also resembles the 1968 Shelby GT350/500.

The 2007 Shelby uses a lot of 1968 Shelby in its styling, but enhanced to create a more macho look. Photo courtesy of Ford Motor Company

The nose of the 1968 Shelby.

Fiberglass hoods were used again, with relocated scoops and air-extractor louvers to aid underhood heat dissipation. They also looked good. Headlight configuration reverted to a single seven-inch unit per side, with Lucas fog lamps mounted inside the grille. The rear body and side scoops were carried over from 1967. The rear tail lights, this time 1965 Thunderbird units, were again sequential. Other embellishments included a chrome rocker panel cover beneath the side body stripe.

The interior used the production Mustang steering wheel. A console that housed two additional gauges was standard equipment. The roll bar, still standard, was encased in vinyl for the convertible.

The Cobra logo has also been used on the SVT Cobra since 1993.

This is the stock wheel cover that was standard on the Shelby. This cover then seemed to be copied by every manufacturer.

9-38 The Shelby interior was the deluxe Mustang but with Shelby embellishments.

The GT350 used a 302 c.i. engine with a single four barrel carburetor.

The High Performance 289, dropped from regular production Mustangs, was deleted from the Shelby as well. In its place a production 302 became standard equipment on the GT350. It used an aluminum intake manifold and a Holley 600 cfm carburetor to boost output to 250hp. The 302 also sported the distinctive Cobra valve covers and air cleaner.

When the 428CJ was introduced, it was also made available on the Shelby. This Shelby was called KR, or King of the Road.

The 428 c.i. for the GT500 was continued from 1967, but with some changes. The expensive dual-quad intake manifold and carburetors were replaced with a single Holley 650 cfm carburetor on an aluminum intake manifold. The 428 c.i. was now rated five horsepower more at 360hp. During the model year, coinciding with the 428CJ's release, the GT500 was dropped and replaced by the GT500KR (King of the Road). The GT500KR had the more powerful 428CJ and came with all the necessary chassis modifications, but the engine was rated at only 355hp.

The suspension remained unchanged from regular production Mustangs but handling was better. This Shelby Mustang used 15x6 inch steel wheels with Goodyear E70x15 tires, and combined with the fiberglass hoods, there was improved weight distribution. The aluminum 15x7 inch Shelby wheels were a popular option.

The GT500KR was clearly the fastest Shelby yet (except for the three 1967 427s), with quarter-mile times easily in the 13-second range.

These Shelby Mustangs were more distinctive than ever before, especially the convertible, so they

The convertible introduced in 1968 had a unique roll bar. The convertible has remained one of the most sought-after Shelby Mustangs.

The 1968 Shelby convertible from the rear.

The 428CJ used on the 1968 Shelby.

were perfectly suited for their targeted buyers. The car provided more than adequate handling, braking, and impressive acceleration in a package that was more attractive and luxurious than regular Mustangs. Production increased to an all-time high of 4,451 units, with about sixty percent being big-block GT500s or GT500KRs.

A point worth considering with the 1968 GT500s is that some of the engines in these cars may be 390s because Ford ran out of 428s at some time during the year and substituted. As is well known, both engines are visually identical, but in terms of true horsepower, the 390 c.i. put out at least 75hp less than the 428 c.i.

1969–70 SHELBY MUSTANG GT350 AND GT500

The GT350 and the GT500 were the most extensively restyled Shelby Mustangs. No longer resembling production Mustangs, they featured a completely restyled nose section, which in many ways presaged the 1971 Mustang. Totally under Ford control, the Shelby Mustangs were no longer the focus of Ford's performance activities, but visually, they continued to convey an overwhelming sense of power and performance.

The 1969 Shelby was totally redesigned. It did not look at all like a Mustang.

The 1969 Shelby featured a completely redesigned fiberglass nose section which resembled the 1971 production Mustang's.

The rear was restyled, too. The same tail lights were used, but the rear spoiler was even more pronounced. The exhaust system used a unique collector in the middle of the rear valence panel.

The nose was lengthened by four inches. Fiberglass was still used for the hood, but the revised grille and bumper necessitated different front fenders, which were also made of fiberglass. Headlights were two seven-inch units with Lucas lamps mounted beneath the front bumper. The hood incorporated five scoops and even the front fenders had a small scoop. A larger side scoop took the place on the Shelby of the simulated side scoop from the production SportsRoofs.

The rear section used 1965 Thunderbird sequential tail lights again, but the rear spoiler was more pronounced. The exhaust system used a unique collector in the middle of the rear valence panel. The large reflective side stripes running the length of the car had either the GT350 or GT500 lettering on the front fender.

The Shelby got a redesigned wheel in 1969. Measuring 15x7 inches, it used an aluminum center with a steel rim. Standard tires were E70x15 but later in the year, the F60xI5 Goodyear Polyglas tires became available instead. At concours shows, all you'll ever see are F60x15s.

The standard GT350 engine was the 290hp 351W. The interior was deluxe Mustang with the high-

9-47 Headlights were two seven-inch units with Lucas lamps mounted beneath the front bumper. There were plenty of scoops on the hood as well, with a total of five on the hood. Even the front fenders had a small scoop.

9-48 From the side, the Shelby resembled the production Mustang, but the side rear scoop was larger than in the regular Mustang.

Basically, the rear was "more" than before.

The interior of the Shelby was just like the interior used with the Mach 1, but with appropriate identification.

back bucket seats and appropriate Shelby identification. The standard console featured a different top that housed two additional gauges. All Shelbys continued to have a roll bar.

Mechanically, these Shelbys were identical to the 1969 Mach 1. The engine for the GT500 was the 428CJ-R, rated at 335hp. The GT350 got the four-barrel version of the 351W. The new 351 Windsor engine, rated at 290hp, used a more efficient aluminum intake manifold and had Ram-Air as well. No Cobra valve covers or air cleaners on either engine were included. The 428CJ did get finned valve covers, however, while the 351W got plain finned aluminum valve covers and a chrome dipstick.

The GT350 came with the 351W engine. This one also has Carroll Shelby's signature on the air cleaner.

The GT500 engine was the 428CJ.

The 1970 Shelby. To help differentiate it from the 1969 car, it featured a Boss 302-type front spoiler and dual stripes on the hood.

Although all of the 1969 Shelby Mustangs were built in 1969, the last in November, not all were sold that year. There were 789 that were updated and sold as 1970 models by having their serial numbers changed. Two black stripes were added on the hood, and a Boss 302-type front spoiler was mounted. In all other respects, they were identical to the 1969 models.

With increased emphasis on the Mach 1s and Bosses, Ford saw no reason to continue promoting the Shelby Mustang, especially as the 1969 model run was not sold within the model year. The Shelby Mustang had made its mark years back, and since 1967, had mainly served as a way to test the innovations of the Ford stylists. It would have been interesting to see what they could have done with a 1971-73 Shelby Mustang model.

1980-82 SHELBY MUSTANG CONVERTIBLES

From 1980 through 1982, Carroll Shelby's company was still a functioning entity. He chose to produce an additional run of 12 convertibles, based on used 1966 Mustang convertibles. Mr. Shelby held the right to use his serial numbers and did so. They could be considered Shelby Mustangs because they were built under Shelby's auspices, but they weren't quite the same thing as those built in 1966.

PROSPECTS

The R cars and the convertibles are the most desirable Shelbys, followed by the 1965 and 1966 models. Originality, authenticity, and condition are of paramount importance, with an extremely small percentage of these cars modified from the original to any great degree. It is important to know that Shelby dealers offered a wide array of mechanical options, such as the Cobra kits. Any Shelby equipped with an exotic intake system, such as a Weber carburetor, is especially valuable.

The only negative that comes along with such desirability and high appreciation is that there is danger of these wonderful cars becoming another commodity for investors to trade in. It's already happened with other makes, where the primary purpose for acquisition is a high return. Like all other Shelby Mustangs, the 1967 cars are in high demand. They do not fetch prices as high as the 1965-66 cars, so are somewhat affordable, but they'll never be less expensive than they are today. Noteworthy are the big-block powered GT500s, as are the extremely rare 427-powered cars. Look for extensive documentation for any 427-powered GT500, as these were dealer installed. For purists, Carroll Shelby's 1967 Shelby Mustangs are the last true Shelby Mustangs worth buying.

With so few Shelby convertibles made, they are showing the fastest appreciation of all 1968 Mustangs. There probably aren't many bargains left, but you never know. The 1968 fastbacks are similar in performance to the 1967 models, so it is a matter of taste. Some prefer the more aggressive look of the 1968 cars, while other enthusiasts prefer the 1967 model because Carroll Shelby still had some control over its production.

The 1969 models are just as much in demand as other Shelby Mustangs are. Their unique styling and the fact that they are the last of the breed make them a good investment. As with the 1968 cars, the convertibles are highly sought after.

2007 FORD SHELBY COBRA GT500

Well, it was bound to happen—the Shelby Mustang is once again available after a 35 year hiatus, under the GT500 moniker. How could anyone doubt it would come back?

The 2007 Shelby is unmistakably related to the Mustang but there are some huge differences. The Mustang GT comes with a 300hp version of the 4.6 liter modular engine, while the GT500's 5.4 liter DOHC supercharged engine puts out 475hp. This is the most powerful factory Mustang ever!

The DOHC 5.4 liter modular engine really puts out the horsepower. It is rated at 475hp. Photo courtesy of Ford Motor Company

The engine uses a cast-iron block, with four-valve cylinder heads, and is force-fed an air and fuel mixture via a screw-type supercharger at 8.5 lbs/inch of boost. Aluminum cylinder heads, piston rings, and bearings sourced from the Ford GT program bring a high level of proven durability to the drivetrain, while upgraded cooling components promise longevity. Powered by SVT camshaft covers are the finishing touch to the engine. The only transmission used is a T-56 six-speed manual.

The GT500 features a MacPherson strut independent front suspension with Reverse L lower control arms, a solid-axle, three-link rear suspension with coil springs, and a Panhard rod for precise control of the rear axle. SVT engineers retuned and upgraded key chassis components such as revised shocks, spring rates, and upgraded stabilizer bars, that help the GT500 stop and turn with the same authority as it goes. Brakes are 14-inch cross-drilled Brembo rotors up front and 13-inch discs in the rear. 19-inch wheels are used with front Goodyear tires measuring 255/45R-19, and rear 285/40R-19.

The Shelby design elements alone are enough to tell the GT500 story, but are not the only visual cues that set this Mustang apart. The reworked front fascia features a functional air splitter, and the unique hood has heat-extraction ducts; these combine to provide improved airflow and aerodynam-

The nose of the GT500 looks really mean. Note the prominent stripes. Photo courtesy of Ford Motor Company

The Shelby GT500 means business. Photo courtesy of Ford Motor Company

From the side, the Shelby GT500 incorporates styling cues from the 1960s. In particular, note the side rear window, the side GT500 stripes, and the snake emblem on the front fenders. Photo courtesy of Ford Motor Company

The Shelby GT500 from the back. Photo courtesy of Ford Motor Company

ics. Revised headlamp insets offer a more aggressive look and result in symmetrical upper and lower grilles.

The unique rear fascia features strakes inspired by the Ford GT's integrated rear airflow diffuser, and a rear spoiler reminiscent of a classic GT500. To mark the collaboration of two Mustang performance icons, the GT500 features Shelby and SVT badging. Continuing the snake logo tradition of past-generation SVT Mustang Cobras, as well as late-model Shelby Mustangs, the fenders each feature an updated design of the Cobra.

For the first time on any SVT Mustang, the front grille features an off-center snake in place of the standard running horse. "GT500" is emblazoned inside the side rocker stripes, and the name "SHELBY" is prominently featured across the rear deck. The SVT logo can be seen on the wheel center caps, a signature SVT location, as well as on the door-sill plates. To top it off, the gas cap medallion between the tail lights reads "Shelby GT500," centered on the Cobra image.

The convertible version of the GT500. A roll bar is not part of the package. All 1965-70 Shelbys were equipped with a roll bar. Photo courtesy of Ford Motor Company

The interior is finished in ebony black leather, including the top of the dash, door panels, and center arm rest. Also in ebony leather are the shift lever, shift boot, and parking-brake handle. SVT Red leather seat and door panel inserts provide a marked contrast to

GT500 striping and a Cobra emblem are part of the identification package on the GT500. Photo courtesy of Ford Motor Company

Both versions of the GT500 are shown here. Photo courtesy of Ford Motor Company

the rest of the leather-trimmed cabin, surrounding the performance enthusiast with luxury and comfort. Snake logos embroidered into the seat backs finish the package.

The Shelby GT500 script and Cobra image are repeated on the steering wheel cap. Behind the wheel are titanium-faced gauges swapped in location so that the tachometer is dominant visually for the driver. The chrome accessories inside the cabin have been replaced with a satin aluminum finish, including the aluminum shift lever knob that is positioned for quick, positive shifts of the six-speed transmission.

All this adds up to a quarter-mile time of 12.5 seconds and a top speed of 160 mph. The GT500 is available in two forms, a two-door coupe and a two-door convertible.

10
1974–1978 Mustang

PRODUCTION

1974

60F 2dr hardtop	177,671
69F 3dr hatchback	74,799
60H 2dr hardtop Ghia	89,477
69R 3dr hatchback Mach 1	44,046
Total	385,993

1975

60F 2dr hardtop	85,155
69F 3dr hatchback	30,038
60H 2dr hardtop Ghia	52,320
69RR 3dr hatchback Mach 1	21,062
Total	188,575

1976

60F 2dr hardtop	78,508
69F 3dr hatchback	62,312
60H 2dr hardtop Ghia	37,515
69R 3dr hatchback Mach 1	9,232
Total	187,567

1977

60F 2dr hardtop	67,783
69R 3dr hatchback	49,161
60H 2dr hardtop Ghia	29,510
69R 3dr hatchback Mach 1	6,719
Total	153,173

1978

60F 2dr hardtop	81,304
69F 3dr hatchback	68,408
60H 2dr hardtop Ghia	34,730
69R 3dr hatchback Mach 1	7,968
Total	192,410

1974

In 1974 the Mustang underwent a severe change. It retained styling cues of the older cars, but with a "new" look. The new styling alienated many Mustang enthusiasts. This is the notchback. Photo courtesy of Ford Motor Company

From the beginning, the Mustang II was envisioned as a way to repeat the fantastic success Ford had enjoyed with the original Mustang. Market research had shown that the youthful buyers, who had bought Mustangs in droves, were now buying cars like the Maverick and Plymouth Duster. A crop of new enthusiasts looking for high performance were opting for the Datsun 240Z and a host of other imports. All these cars had one thing in common: They were a lot smaller than the first-generation Mustang.

Intended to be a very different car, the Mustang II managed to incorporate many of the original's styling cues. The most obvious similarity was in the front grille and side sculpturing. During its five years of production, the Mustang II's basic styling on both the hardtop and the fastback did not change. Ford made no convertibles.

The Mustang II ceased to be a pony car and could now be classified as a subcompact. Ford had effectively abandoned that market segment to GM's Camaro and Firebird. By 1977, the Camaro outsold the Mustang II. The Mustang II competed instead against cars like GM's Skyhawk, Starfire, and Monza—you remember them, don't you?

The hatchback design looked a little better. This one has the removable T-Top roof. Photo courtesy of Ford Motor Company

Overall, the Mustang II did not prove to be the success Ford hoped for. Sales during the first year were respectable with 385,994 cars sold. The main cause was the first OPEC oil embargo which caused the price of gas to go up considerably. Any car that looked small, and therefore received more miles per gallon, was snapped up by the frantic public.

Despite the fact that the Mustang II shared the front engine and rear-wheel drive configuration of the first-generation Mustang, in many ways it was quite different. The front suspension was redesigned, and the front springs were now located between the control arms rather than above the upper A-arm, which improved ride quality. Another major difference was the use of a front subframe designed to isolate the engine from the rest of the chassis. This was necessary because the Mustang II's standard four-cylinder engine vibrated quite a bit. Other improvements included the use of rack-and-pinion steering, standard front disc brakes, staggered shock rear suspension, and a standard four-speed manual transmission.

The standard engine throughout the Mustang II's production was a 2300 cc (140 c.i.) inline four-cylinder engine. It sported features such as a single overhead cam and a crossflow cylinder head with canted valves. It pumped out a meager 88hp, clearly not enough for a car approaching 3,000 pounds. The optional engine for the 1974 model year was a German-built 2.8 liter V-6 (171 c.i.). A good little engine, its 105hp was again not enough for the Mustang II. In fact, when the car first came out, it was panned by the automotive press for being too slow. There was no V-8 option on the 1974 model—the only year that this awful thing happened!

The Ghia took the place of the Grande as the luxury model for the Mustang II. Ford acquired the Italian Ghia design studios in 1970, and used the badge to lend an exotic, European flavor to the car. Ghia engineers did contribute to the initial design but the Ghia Mustang itself was pure Detroit.

For performance, or at least the looks of performance, the Mach 1 was available on the fastback body. The fastback, by the way, had become a hatchback.

113

Following the Mustang tradition, the options list was long and full of creature comforts. One nice feature was the use of a more informative dash: A tachometer and fuel and temperature gauges were standard. Unfortunately, seats with a reclining adjustment were still years away.

1975–1976

In 1976, Ford released the Mustang II Cobra II. It was the hot Mustang for 1976 and at a quick glance, it looks a little like a 1966 Shelby Cobra. Shelby enthusiasts at the time threw their arms in the air in exasperation.

The year 1975 saw few changes. The Ghia got an opera window, the rage of the mid-seventies luxury set. Of greater significance was the availability of the 302 V-8. It was available with an automatic transmission and rated at only 140hp, but this engine was a giant step forward. Typical 0–60 mph times were in the ten-second range, and quarter-mile times in the 17-second range. *Road & Track*, which has traditionally panned American-made cars, had to grudgingly admit that the V-8 Mach 1 wasn't a bad car.

The introduction of the Cobra II in 1976 had a very positive impact on the Ford image. This was basically a cosmetic package available for the fastback body. Ford offered three colors: white with blue stripes, blue with white stripes, and black with gold stripes, the last choice emulating the Shelby Hertz cars.

The Cobra II package consisted of front and rear spoilers, a simulated hood scoop, rear side window louvers, rocker panel stripes, aluminum wheels with RWL tires, and color-keyed mirrors. Cobra snake decals were affixed on each front fender, while a Cobra emblem was placed in the center of the blacked-out grille.

The Cobra II's standard engine was the V-6, and the 302 V-8 was optional. Only the V-8 Cobra IIs should be considered by collectors. The use of the Cobra name infuriated Shelby Mustang owners and enthusiasts. The Cobra name had always invoked images of tremendous power and performance, and it was felt that the Cobra II just didn't live up to the name. This may be true, but Ford owned the rights to the name, and that name improved the Mustang's image and increased sales.

Another cosmetic package available in 1976 was the Stallion model, which coincided with similar offerings from Ford's Maverick and Pinto. If you don't know what a Maverick or Pinto is, you haven't missed anything.

This Mustang had better ergonomics than the older cars. The hatchback rear was very useful in this 1977 Cobra II.

The original Shelby Mustang Cobras had a small two-inch fender emblem. The Cobra II had a ten-inch version. If small was good, was bigger better?

1977–1978

Only minor styling changes were made in 1977. The Ghia could be had with the Ghia Sports Group (another cosmetic package), and notchbacks could be ordered with a pop-up sunroof. Fastbacks

In 1977, the Cobra II package included additional colors, like this one that is black with gold stripes.

were available with a T-top, while the Cobra II was now available in additional color schemes, white with red and white with green. The Sports Performance Package finally added the four-speed manual transmission to the 302 V-8, transforming the Mustang into a decent performer by seventies standards.

The year 1978 was the last for the Mustang II, by this time a tired design. The Cobra II got a rear window louver, similar to the Boss 302's Sports Slats, that was attractive but the garish new side stripes didn't help.

KING COBRA

The last cosmetic permutation of the Mustang II was the King Cobra, which borrowed several features from Pontiac's Firebird Trans Am. A large snake decal graced a hood that included a non-functioning rear-facing hood scoop. Instead of using the Cobra II's front spoiler, the King Cobra

115

In 1978, Ford modified the Cobra II look. Spoilers, scoops, stripes, window slats—you name it and the Cobra II had it. Problem was that the car didn't deliver on performance.

This is a beautifully restored example of a 1978 Cobra II. It takes a lot of guts to drive one; a real "car guy" would rather drive an older Mustang than a new Mustang II.

Sitting inside a Mustang II still feels pretty good. This 1978 Cobra II has the T-Top roof.

The last of the Mustang II performance cars was the King Cobra. Actually, it does look good. Just tastefully done striping accented the car.

The hood decal might be too much, but remember, the Pontiac Firebird sold a lot of Trans Ams with a similar hood decal. The 5.0 on the hood scoop was the first time that Ford used 5.0 to describe the 302 c.i. V-8.

was equipped with a front air dam. It also had rear wheel well spoilers, again borrowed from Pontiac.

The King Cobra came with the 302 engine, four-speed transmission, power brakes, power steering (variable-ratio), and wire style aluminum wheels, as well as the Rallye package that provided heavy-duty springs, adjustable shocks, and a rear sway bar. The T-top was optional.

PROSPECTS

For collectors, 1974 has little to offer. The cars were so underpowered that they weren't much fun to drive. Handling and braking were actually pretty good, but lack of power made it hard to take advantage of it.

If you have your heart set on a second-generation Mustang, the King Cobra is probably the best bet, followed by the V-8 Cobra IIs and Mach 1s. You may not see much appreciation in these cars, however.

Even though second-generation Mustangs haven't been highly regarded, they have developed a decent following. These cars are becoming an increasing presence at car shows. Unfortunately, they are constantly being compared to the first-generation Mustangs, which is natural, but isn't really fair. Comparing second-generation Mustangs to other mid- to late-1970s offerings is actually more appropriate and here the Mustang II has shown itself a superior car and a good performer.

11
1979–1993 Mustang

PRODUCTION

1979 Mustang

66B 2dr sedan	156,666
61R 3dr hatchback	120,535
66H 2dr sedan Ghia	56,351
61H 3dr hatchback Ghia	36,384
Total	369,936
All with 5.0L	47,568
Pace car replicas	10,478

1980 Mustang

66B 2dr sedan	128,893
61R 3dr hatchback	98,497
66H 2dr sedan Ghia	23,647
61H 3dr hatchback Ghia	20,285
Total	271,322

1981 Mustang

66B 2dr sedan	77,458
66H 2 dr sedan Ghia	13,422

61R 3dr hatchback	77,399
61H 3dr hatchback Ghia	14,273
Total	182,552

1982 Mustang

66B 2dr sedan L/GL	45,316
66H 2 dr sedan GLX	5,828
61R 3dr hatchback GL	45,901
61R 3dr hatchback GLX	9,926
61H 3dr hatchback GT	23,447
Total	130,418
P16F GT/GLX 5.0L hatchback	35,435

1983 Mustang

66B 2dr sedan	33,201
66B 2dr convertible	23,438
61B 3dr hatchback	64,234
Total	120,873
P28F GT 5.0L hatchback	27,995
P26F GLX 5.0L sedan	1,170
P27F GT/GLX convertible	6,369
P28W Turbo GT hatchback	556

1984 Mustang

66B 2dr sedan	37,680	
66B 2dr convertible	17,600	(includes 2dr GT convertible, 6,256)
61B 3dr hatchback	86,200	(includes 3dr GT convertible, 32,914)
Total	141,480	(includes 2dr convertible and 3dr hatchback Turbo GT, 3,798)

1984 Mustang 20th Anniversary Edition

3dr Turbo GT	350
3dr 5.0l GT	3,333
2dr convertible Turbo GT	104
2dr convertible 5.0l GT	1,213
Ford VIP convertibles	15

Ford of Canada (total)	245
Total	5,260
P28M GT/LX 5.0L hatchback	29,142
P26M LX 5.0L sedan	1,395
P27M GT/LX 5.0L convertible	7,643
P28W Turbo GT hatchback	3,241
P27W Turbo GT convertible	731

1984–86 Mustang SVO

1984	4,263
1985	1,925
1986	3,314
Total	9,502

1985 Mustang

66B 2dr sedan	56,781
66B 2dr convertible	15,110
61B 3dr hatchback	84,623
Total	156,514
P28M GT/LX 5.0L hatchback	39,460
P26M LX 5.0L sedan	2,284

1986 Mustang

66B 2dr sedan	83,774
66B 2dr convertible	22,946
61B 3dr hatchback	117,690
Total	224,410
P28M GT/LX 5.0 hatchback	43,016
P26M LX 5.0L sedan	2,825
P27M GT/LX 5.0L convertible	11,265

1987 Mustang

66B 2dr sedan	43,257
66B 2dr convertible	32,074

61B 3dr hatchback	94,441
Total	159,145
P40E LX 5.0L sedan	4,888
P41E LX 5.0L hatchback	9,642
P44E LX 5.0L convertible	2,073
P42E GT hatchback	37,056
P45E GT convertible	10,451

1988 Mustang

66B 2dr sedan	53,221
66B 2dr convertible	32,074
61B 3dr hatchback	125,930
Total	211,225
P40E LX 5.0L sedan	5,568
P41E LX 5.0L hatchback	16,331
P44E LX 5.0L convertible	5,188
P42E GT hatchback	50,282
P45E GT convertible	18,158

1989 Mustang

66B 2dr sedan	50,560
66B 2dr convertible	42,244
61B 3dr hatchback	116,965
Total	209,769
P40E LX 5.0L sedan	10,528
P41E LX 5.0L hatchback	24,734
P44E LX 5.0L convertible	10,575
P42E GT hatchback	40,231
P45E GT convertible	19,417

1990 Mustang

66B 2dr sedan	22,503
66B 2dr convertible	26,958
61B 3dr hatchback	78,728
Total	128,189

P40E LX 5.0L sedan	7,905
P41E LX 5.0L hatchback	17,409
P44E LX 5.0L convertible	9,692
P42E GT hatchback	33,639
P45E GT convertible	12,252

1991 Mustang

66B 2dr sedan	19,447
66B 2dr convertible	21,513
61B 3dr hatchback	57,777
Total	98,737

P40E LX 5.0L sedan	7,299
P41E LX 5.0L hatchback	12,717
P44E LX 5.0L convertible	7,850
P42E GT hatchback	24,677
P45E GT convertible	8,852

1992 Mustang

66B 2dr sedan	15,717
66B 2dr convertible	23,470
61B 3dr hatchback	40,093
Total	79,280

2dr convertible Vibrant Red	2,019
P40E LX 5.0L sedan	5,346
P41E LX 5.0L hatchback	8,671
P44E LX 5.0L convertible	6,606
P42E GT hatchback	14,065
P44E GT convertible	5,823

1993 Mustang

66B 2dr sedan	24,851
66B 2dr convertible	27,300
61B 3dr hatchback	62,077
Total	114,228

2dr convertible Canary Yellow	1,503
2dr convertible Oxford White	1,500

3dr hatchback Cobra	5,100 (includes 107 Cobra R models)
P40E LX 5.0L sedan	7,135
P41E LX 5.0L hatchback	9,376
P44E LX 5.0L convertible	6,382
P42E GT hatchback	14,459
P45E GT convertible	6,535

1979

The 1979 Mustang hit the market with a bang. Over 369,000 were sold in the first year alone. The Mustang no longer looked like the Mustangs of old, and just as well, too. This is the Pace car.

The third-generation Mustang was a total departure from the Mustang II. There was no attempt to connect it with past Mustangs in terms of styling, but proportionally, it still had the long hood and short deck styling that distinguished the first-generation Mustangs. Initially this third-generation Mustang was available as a two-door sedan and three-door fastback, with the convertible becoming available during the 1983 model year.

In terms of size, this Mustang was larger than the Mustang II. The wheelbase was lengthened four inches, to 100.4 inches, and it stood on a wider track, yet it was lighter. As a reflection of the increased importance of aerodynamics, its coefficient of drag (CD) was twenty-five percent less than the Mustang II's at 0.44 (0.46 for the sedan), a good figure by 1979 standards. For comparison, a baseball has a CD of 0.45, a bullet 0.25, and a 747 jet airliner 0.02. Improved aerodynamics have been partially responsible for the current Mustang GT's top speed, which was clocked at 150 mph.

The new Mustang's styling became thoroughly modern. Its sloped nose has been widely copied. Although the third-generation Mustang's styling received minor yearly updates, the styling remained close to the second-generation's body shell and platform. A significant change that occurred with the 1987 models incorporated Ford's aero look, but the Mustang was essentially the same car it had been in 1979. The design became somewhat dated by 1993, but the original design had a staying power that was reflected by production figures.

Other first- and second-generation Mustangs had been based on other Ford products. This Mustang used the Fairmont platform, known as the Fox platform, but bore no resemblance to the boxy Fairmont sedan. The front suspension used McPherson struts to replace the conventional upper A-arms, and the coil spring was located on the lower arm and on the chassis. This type of suspension was found in many imported cars of the time and had the advantage of being cheaper to manufacture. The rear suspension used coil springs with four bar links to locate the rear axle. A front anti-roll bar was standard, while V-8 Mustangs and those equipped with the optional handling suspension also came with a rear anti-roll bar.

Ford exerted a great effort to make the 1979 Mustang a car that would handle well. The Mustang was available with the Michelin 190/65R 390 TRX tires as an option, which in 1979 were considered state of the art. The 65 series tires had to be mounted on a specially sized wheel rim, measuring 15.4 by 5.9 inches. When combined with specially calibrated anti-roll bars, shocks, and springs, the Mustang did indeed handle well. The TRX tires remained available until 1984.

Four engines were available on the 1979 Mustang. The standard engine was the same 2.3 liter four-cylinder available with the Mustang II that pumped out a paltry 88hp. The 2.8 liter V-6 was optional. The performance engines were a turbocharged 2.3 liter four-cylinder and the familiar 302 V-8 5.0 liter in two-barrel carburetor trim. By this time, engine size was generally referred to in metric terms, so as liters rather than cubic inches.

The standard engine with the Pace car was the 2.3l Turbo four cylinder engine. The engine turned out to be a failure and by 1981, Ford had pulled it from the Mustang's options list. The 5.0l was a much better engine.

Ford promoted the turbocharged four-cylinder as an important new innovation, but basically this engine was an attempt to combine the high mileage characteristics of a small engine with the high horsepower of a V-8. Rated at 132hp (only eight horsepower less than the 302) it actually proved to be a dud. Although Ford strengthened the engine internally, it had a high failure rate. Turbo technology has come a long way since 1979, but most turbocharged engines still suffer from turbo lag and do require special maintenance. The turbocharged four-cylinder was standard equipment on the third-generation Cobra Mustang, available only as a fastback. Also included on the Cobra were the TRX suspension package and appropriate identification. A large snake hood decal was an option.

A more reliable choice was the optional 302 V-8 engine. In two-barrel, single-exhaust form, it was rated at 140hp. Yet even at this low output, the 302 V-8 was a bit too much for the rear suspension, and severe axle hop and tramp were evident under drag starts.

During the year, the 2.8 liter German built V-6 was replaced with the now old 200 c.i. inline six.

Along with the performance Cobra, the Ghia models were available as the luxury Mustangs, in either two- or three-door form.

PACE CAR REPLICA

A special run of 10,478 replica Pace car Mustangs was assembled to commemorate the specially prepared Mustangs chosen to pace the Indy 500. These were built between April and July, 1979. The Pace cars were all powered by the 5.0 liter V-8, but the replicas had either the 2.3 liter turbocharged four-cylinder or the 5.0 liter V-8. The last time Mustang had qualified to pace the Indy 500 was in 1964.

Naturally, the Pace cars had to look different. They were all finished in pewter with black trim and orange-red-black striping. "Mustang" was spelled out in large orange and red block letters along both sides of the hood, and red-orange striping with galloping ponies were used on the sides of the car. Other decals were included in the purchase price and could be installed at the owner's discretion. The decals included an "Official Pace Car 63rd Annual Indianapolis 500" decal, the race date, May 27, 1979, and the Indianapolis shield.

The Pace Car package also included halogen headlights with removable bulbs, front air-dam with foglights, a rear decklid spoiler, a non-functional hood scoop (facing backwards), blacked-out trim, a special front grille, dual orange molding on blacked out bumpers, Recaro seats in black-and-white trim, a leather-wrapped steering wheel, and engine-turned dash. The package also offered a sunroof, center console with digital clock, AM/FM stereo radio with cassette or 8-track, interval wipers, dual-remote outside mirrors, and a special Indianapolis Motor Speedway rectangular plaque. All in all, this was a fairly loaded package.

Three specially designed and engineered cars were used at Indy in 1979 as pace and parade vehicles. The 5.0 liter V-8 engines were used, but with modifications. A Holley (R-6989A) from a 1973 Ford was used on an aluminum high-rise intake manifold and a chrome air cleaner from a 1974 Ford police car. Internally, 1971 351 Windsor heads with 1.84 inches intake and 1.54 inches exhaust valves were used, along with 1969 Boss 302 connecting rods and a forged-steel crankshaft.

The rest of the valvetrain included 289 HiPo valve springs and a 1970 Boss 302 solid lifter camshaft. Pistons were forged aluminum TRW with Speed Pro rings. Jack Roush put the engines together. All three cars used modified C-4 automatic transmissions and were fitted with special T-tops by Cars and Concepts.

Two of the original three Pace cars are currently at the Roush Transportation Museum.

1980–81

The years 1980-81 were a low point for the Mustang, at least from the performance standpoint. The 5.0l engine was dropped from the options list and replaced with a 4.2l version, rated at 119hp. The decrease in displacement was accomplished by reducing the bore from 4.00 to 3.68 inches. The 4.2l was available only with the automatic transmission.

The same engine lineup was carried over for 1981, although the turbo four-cylinder was deleted.

Although the 4.2l engine looked the same as the 5.0l, it used considerably lighter internal parts and block. Modification for more power was not recommended. The crankshaft was not strong enough at higher rpms.

You rarely see 1980–81 Mustangs at car shows today. This period was the worst in the Mustang's history. Even the 5.0l V-8 was withdrawn and instead, an anemic 4.2l took its place. Ford was concentrating on meeting the demands of a changing market and devoted few resources to the performance Mustang. Photo courtesy of Ford Motor Company

1982

The coverage Ford got in the performance area with the new Mach 1 series, the Boss Mustangs, and the Shelby Mustangs, had sounded the death knell for the Mustang GT in 1969. Then, after a 12-year hiatus, Ford decided to reintroduce the GT. In 1982, the Mach 1s, the Bosses, and the Shelbys were all considered defunct, so it was hoped that bringing back one of them would have the same effect as the releasing of a new car.

The 5.0l V-8 was used as the standard engine but it sported a somewhat larger two-barrel carbure-

127

Hope at last! Prodded by the successful downsized 1982 Chevrolet Camaro and Pontiac Firebird, Ford re-released the 1982 Mustang GT. It was the right move, because it gave enthusiasts something to cheer about.

tor, an aluminum intake manifold, and a slightly better single exhaust system. This engine was rated at 157hp, so it was necessary for Ford to install rear traction bars to help control rear wheel hop. The GT also featured the front air dam, rear spoiler, and front-facing simulated hood scoop. The handsome TRX wheels and tires were also standard.

The 302 was also available on all other Mustang models, which included the L, GL, and GLX (the Ghia nameplate had been dropped).

Despite its efforts, Ford couldn't seem to stop the Mustang's production slide. Bear in mind that it had to react to the newly restyled Camaro and Firebird. The new GM F-body cars were 10 inches longer, three inches wider, and 400 pounds heavier than the Mustang. While the new F-body car had been downsized, it was still bigger than the Mustang. The Camaro and Firebird had a lot of styling cues that would be seen later on the 1984 Corvette. So while the Camaro and Firebird were enjoying increased sales, the Mustang barely held on.

It was not practical for Ford to do anything drastic, but they had a lot of good parts left over from other projects. Careful blending and mixing could be used to make the Mustang appear newly designed too. All the Ghia models were dropped and replaced by the L, GL, and GLX series. The new nomenclature became more in tune with what Ford's European and Japanese competitors were doing anyway. The top-of-the-line car was no longer the Cobra; its place was taken by the new GT.

The new GT exhibited clean, crisp lines, not at all like the Mustang II Cobra II. Clearly, it was the right Mustang for the time.

General Motors, with the newly restyled Camaro and Firebird, still relied on V-8 power. The top Camaro put out 165hp, and there was nothing in Ford's Mustang product bin that would match it. The experiment with the 2.3 liter turbocharged four cylinder had ended in dismal failure, so the next best thing was to resurrect the 5.0 liter (302 c.i.d.) V-8.

The 5.0 liter was re-introduced after having been put to rest in 1979. In actuality, Ford really didn't have much to do to the engine. Although the engine was re-released with improved output, it was available with only a two-barrel carburetor, single-exhaust, and a slightly better camshaft. Still, the 157hp and a 400 pound weight advantage against the Camaro/Firebird proved to be enough.

The Mustang was now heralded as "the fastest car in America."

1983

1983 brought additional development and progress. The Mustang front end was restyled, while the rear got European-looking tail lamps. A third body style joined the line-up—an eye-catching convertible. The convertible was also available as a GT, sporting all the GT features: TRX wheels, graphics, and, of course, the 5.0l V-8 engine.

The 5.0l was updated to 175hp through the use of a Holley 600 cfm four-barrel carburetor. Wheel hop remained a problem despite the fact that the 1983 GT came with traction bars (as did the 1982 GTs). Momentum did not stop with the 1984 Mustangs, either. In fact, the Mustang quickly became a serious performance car. The Mustang GT continued to sport the 175hp version of the 302 HO, but only with the five-speed manual transmission. Factory literature also listed a 205 hp version with dual exhausts, but this particular engine never appeared that year. Mustang GTs with the automatic transmission got an EFI 302 HO rated at 165 hp.

The grille was changed slightly for 1983-84, and the Mustang got more popular as well. It was more powerful, too.

New for 1983 was the convertible Mustang. The last time a convertible had been offered was in 1973. It was the right move, as convertible Mustangs made a huge difference in sales. Shown here is a GT version.

Ford released the GT Turbo again in 1984. A handsome car to be sure, but not many takers. Ford would try once more with the Turbo engine, this time with the 1984 SVO.

The 2.3l Turbo four cylinder engine made a comeback in 1983-84 in the GT Turbo Mustang. It was a much improved, more reliable engine than the 1979 engine. The problem was that no one wanted it; the 5.0l Mustang kept getting more powerful and so did sales.

The year 1983 was one of change for the Mustang. This was well and good for the enthusiast—the GT had more power in 1983, for example. Unfortunately, the improved performance was not widely appreciated and sales continued to slide, hitting the lowest totals since the Mustang's inception in 1964. Even its archrival, the Camaro, outsold the Mustang.

The Mustang also looked a little different in 1983. The new front-end treatment and rear tail light treatment, changed the visual effect. It was also reported that the new nose reduced aerodynamic drag by 2.5%. The GT's hood scoop changed ends as well; this time the opening faced the rear. Otherwise, the Mustang was unchanged.

SPECIALS

A new model joined the line-up halfway through 1983—the Turbo GT. This was the same 2.3 liter Turbo that was fitted in the Thunderbird Turbo Coupe. It included most of the GT options, except for air conditioning and automatic transmission. The T-5 five-speed transmission was included as standard equipment.

The 2.3l Turbo GT, rated at 145hp, was superior to Ford's earlier turbocharging attempt. The engine featured electronic fuel injection, and its earlier reliability problems had been licked.

A problem that emerged was that no one really liked the car. The 5.0l was cheaper, and it was better. The engine, no matter how good, had two things going against it. First, it was small (as compared to the V-8). And second, it suffered from turbo lag. Engineering was not able to overcome the lag. This is one of the reasons why Ford chose to invest heavily in supercharging thereafter.

1984

This was the year that the downward sales trend finally reversed itself, as the Mustang started to inch up. Sales for the archrival Camaro on the other hand, had reached stratospheric proportions, at 261,591 total cars sold. It would take some time before the Mustang caught up.

This is a 1984 Mustang GT.

Ford had decided to give the Mustang a shot in the arm. The power rating for 1984 remained the same, 175hp, but Ford got busy working on other areas of the car. In fact, an upgraded engine was in the works for the second half of 1984, but delays held up production of the engine until the 1985 model year.

It is interesting to note that the long options lists that allowed for some individualization started to grow shorter on the Mustang. Fewer options and limited color choices became the norm.

20TH ANNIVERSARY EDITION MUSTANG

One Mustang model that became an immediate collectible made its appearance in 1984. The 20th Anniversary Edition Mustangs were intended to include the best the Mustang tradition had to offer. All were GT, three-door coupes and convertibles, painted Oxford White (Code 9L) with Canyon Red interiors. Engine choices consisted of either the 5.0l or the Turbo GT four-cylinder. The 20th Anniversary Edition cars also came with the articulated sports seats, like the SVOs discussed later in the chapter, but without the adjustable lumbar support. The rest of the package included a special lower panel tape treatment with GT350 letters and numerals (let's upset those Shelby owners again!), and original Mustang fender emblems.

The 20th Anniversary Edition car also had a rocker panel tape treatment with G.T. 350 lettering,

As it turned out, 1984 was a big year for the Mustang, with lots of different models to choose from. This is the best known: the GT-350 model which celebrated the 20th anniversary of the Mustang.

The 20th Anniversary special also celebrated the Shelby cars, with its G.T. 350 side stripe. It was available as a convertible or a hatchback.

red molding going around the entire car, and two original type 1965 front fender emblems. Two 20th Anniversary dash panel badges were part of the interior indentification. The first of these, a horseshoe medallion, was located on the passenger's side of the dash. Three or four months after purchase, the owner was sent a form to fill out so that the second medallion could be obtained. This one read "Limited Edition" followed by a serial number (unrelated to the car's VIN) and below that, the owner's name.

This model also had the distinction of being the first to have the Quadra-Shock rear suspension system (except for the SVO) as an option. The system used four shock absorbers at the rear which did a much better job than the previous traction bars. It was also possible to obtain the TRX suspension in 1984.

1985

The base Mustang was the LX model, in either a two-door sedan or a three-door hatchback. Power steering and power brakes were now standard features, in addition to AM/FM stereo, dual-covered visor mirrors, interval wipers, 16-ounce carpeting, and a center console on the 3-door models.

The instrumentation on all Mustangs included oil pressure, ammeter, coolant temperature, a resettable trip odometer, and a tachometer. Optional engines on the LX model were the 3.8 V-6 and

1985 was a big year for the Mustang GT. Ford got serious with the GT as the car got a big jolt in the horsepower department.

automatic transmission, or the 5.0l H.O. V-8. The 5.0l H.O. V-8 could be had with either a five-speed manual or an automatic transmission.

In terms of exterior trim, the 1985 Mustang borrowed from the SVO (or vice-versa). GTs got new blackout trim, as well as paint and tape treatment on the hood and decklid. The large GT letters on the hood let the car's original paint color show through, and GT letters were part of the side molding in front of the rear tires. This side molding was part of the urethane protection treatment. A rear spoiler was standard on the GT hatchback.

The standard Mustang engine was the 88hp 2.3l four-cylinder with a four-speed manual or a three-speed automatic transmission. The 3.8l V-6 was optional. Rated at 120hp, it came only with the SelectShift automatic transmission.

The 5.0l V-8 was where all the action was in 1985. The engine had gone from 175hp to 210hp. The aluminum intake manifold and four-barrel carburetor was basically unchanged. It would, however, be the last year for that setup. For 1985, Ford added a choke pull-down diaphragm. Otherwise, the intake system remained unchanged.

The interior of the 1985 Mustang GT.

Ford decided to go with a stainless-steel exhaust header system. Although the factory system had lots of built-in compromises, it was nevertheless a system that was worth up to 10hp over a cast-iron manifold system. For 1985, the exhaust headers fed a single catalytic converter, and then the outlets formed a dual exhaust system. True duals would not show up until 1986. Even so, the bulk of the 35hp gain in 1985 can be attributed to the exhaust system.

To take advantage of the intake and exhaust system, Ford decided to introduce a hydraulic roller lifter camshaft. Roller lifters, besides allowing for more cam lift, are superior to flat tappets. In addition, Ford made some changes to the blocks to make it easier to change roller lifters in the front and rear of the block. The 1985 5.0l V-8 also benefited from the use of forged pistons. The 1985 pistons have thicker ring lands, which means improved heat transfer to the cylinder walls.

As for the automatic versions of the engine, two basic versions were available for 1985. The first is a 165hp CFI (Central Fuel Injected). It is basically the version used in 1984. The version that was introduced later was rated at 180hp. It benefited from the stainless-steel exhaust headers and the rest of the updated exhaust system. Both versions used the aluminum intake, which was really the same one used on the 1979 carbureted two-barrel 5.0l V-8s, and a regular, non-roller camshaft.

New Teflon-lined ball joints were introduced in 1985; the front stabilizer bar's main bushing were Teflon lined; and the rubber end links were replaced by firmer urethane units.

In addition, a Handling Suspension package was available on the LX. It included the Quadra-Shock rear, quick-ratio steering, revised spring and bushing rates, larger anti-roll bars, and special struts and shocks.

The 14x5 inch stamped steel wheel was standard on the 2.3l. An option was a 14x5.5 inch styled road wheel. LX models with the 5.0l V-8 used a 14x5.5 inch cast-aluminum styled road wheel along with P205/70RVR14 tires. Later in the model year, the new ten-hole 15x7 inch became mandatory with the LX, along with the P225/60VR15 Gatorback Goodyear tires and T-5 transmission.

The Gatorbacks and the ten-hole rims were standard on the GT models from the beginning of the model year.

1985 Mustang Twister II

New for 1985 was the limited run of the 1985 Twister II Mustang. This was basically a standard 1985 Mustang GT with a decal package applied by the Kansas City District Sales office. The package consisted of exterior Twister II decals, a bronze dash plate, which read "1985 Limited Edition TWISTER II, Kansas City District, October 1984." Also included were an alabaster coaster, which read "1985 Limited Edition TWISTER II, Kansas City District," and a press package. This featured a press release about the 1985 Twister II. It is possible that not all cars received the press package.

The large Twister II decals were the distinguishing feature of the Twister II Mustang. Photo courtesy of Brad Bowling

In addition, an original Twister II had the DSO code of 53, the scheduled build month of October 1984, and the VIN fell in the following ranges: 109800-109899, 110300-110399, or 112200-112299. Most of the Twister II cars came in Jalapena Red (2R). However, they were also produced in two or possibly three other colors—Oxford White (9L), Medium Canyon Red Metallic (2A), and possibly Silver Metallic (1E).

Total production was 76 hatchbacks and 14 convertibles, for a total of 90 cars.

1986

There is little to distinguish between the 1985 and 1986 Mustangs (shown). However, there was an important change made to the engine of the 1986 and later Mustangs—it was the first year of the fuel injection system.

For the first time, a sequential electronic multipoint fuel injection (SEFI) was used on the 5.0l engine, including those backed up by an automatic transmission in 1986. The SEFI system used a speed density system, which had a 58 mm, 541 cfm throttle body with eight individual (19 lb/hr) fuel injector nozzles. The difference between a speed density and a mass air flow system is that the mass air flow system allows for additional engine modifications without the usual drivability problems that are evident with a speed density system. Also part of the mass air flow system is a 23.3 gallon-per-hour electric fuel pump located inside the gas tank. All Mustangs went to a mass air flow system in 1989.

Also new for 1986 was a stiffened engine block. It had thicker decks and cylinder walls, which helped the new piston rings seal in the combustion pressure. In addition, the block was cast in semi-siamese fashion—only the upper bore walls are fully coolant-jacketed, while the bottom of the cylinders are cast with solid iron. The block weighed 126 lbs.

The exhaust system was new too. This was a true dual exhaust system, with dual catalytic converters and a single muffler per side. In typical Ford fashion, the system also incorporated an H-pipe in the engine pipe.

A different cylinder head was used: part E6AE-6049-AA. It had a smaller, kidney-shaped combustion chamber that had the unfortunate propensity of shrouding the valves, and thus lowering power output. This head was also used on the 1986-91 passenger cars and other Ford applications. Consequently, the engine rated at only 200hp. For 1987, Ford went back to the open-chamber design: part E7TE-6049-PA or E5TE-6049-PA.

All models used the 6.75 inch rear axle, except those powered by the 5.0l engine. These were equipped with the 8.8 inch rear and a Traction-Lok. The 8.8 inch rear was much stronger than the 7.5 inch rear.

1984–86 SVO OVERVIEW

The Mustang SVO, built from 1984-86, was an attempt by Ford to lift the Mustang up into competition with cars like the Porsche. The 2.3l Turbo four cylinder engine did a credible job in the performance arena but in the final analysis, the market was not ready for such a Mustang.

The big news in 1984 was the SVO Mustang. It was quite a step for Ford, as the car was designed to deliver superior performance while appealing to a more sophisticated buyer. The design was based on the Mustang, but was supposed to exude a polished, elegant image. The car had to give the perception that it wasn't really a Mustang, because it cost fifty percent more than the Mustang GT. The Mustang GT cost around $10,000 and the SVO, $16,000. Did the SVO achieve its goal? It can be argued that it did not.

There is no doubt that the SVO had power, and this made it difficult to hide the 2.3l four cylinder engine's origins. The engine used a crossflow head design, a good thing to be sure, but then it was limited by its two valves and single-overhead cam. At high rpm, the engine had a tendency to make a lot of noise. With turbocharging, a lot of the 2.3l four cylinder engine's limitations could be glossed over. It wasn't forgotten either that the 5.0l V-8 makes more power than the 2.3l four, and it weighs only 60-70 pounds more.

Unfortunately, the main competitors to the SVO were German and Japanese cars whose engines used a modern four-valve dual-overhead cam cylinder head. These engines had a propensity to rev and were reliable, too. It would have been much better for the SVO to have a special four-valve cylinder head, dual camshafts, and turbocharging. The case could then have been made that the SVO was different enough from the regular Mustang to be worth the extra money.

Ford had hoped that the SVO would sell considerably better than it did. The Mustang SVO was launched in the fall of 1983 as a 1984 model, with the model scheduled to be discontinued at the end of the 1986 model year. This is a point that often missed about the SVO. It might have to been a phenomenal success had production continued past the planned model three years.

A biplane rear spoiler, 16 inch wheels, and dual exhausts were all part of the SVO.

There are many reasons for the SVO's lack of success. The following information was found in internal company documents from Ford and provides a story that is not generally known.

It shows that unfortunately, Ford wasn't ready to deal head-on with its German and Japanese competitors.

About 3,700 units were built to dealer orders in the third and fourth quarters of 1983, and by January of 1984, dealer stocks were at 3,100 total. This 3,100 figure represented a 428 day supply of the car, which by all accounts was pretty low. Ford had planned to build 8,000 SVO Mustangs and believed, incorrectly, that the pricing of the car wouldn't adversely affect sales in the high-technology segment of the market. When lined up against the comparably equipped Mustang GT, the SVO cost $5,300 more, including $1,700 which was not supported by features or equipment.

Unfortunately, dealers estimated the cars were overpriced by $2,000-3,000. So the SVO's price was lowered by making five of the major options standard (air conditioning, power windows, AM/FM stereo with cassette, power locks, and floor mats) and adding a Competition Preparation Option. The problem was that the price, despite the add-ons, was still way too high.

Production delays at launch also resulted in very limited availability of the car until late November, well after most of the introductory PR and advertising had peaked. Only a few cars were available for sale by the end of September when the SVO was featured on the cover of Motor Trend and Road & Track. There were only 123 units in dealer inventories by the end of October.

Prevailing conditions also were not favorabe to the SVO. Sales programs offered the Mustang GT and Thunderbird Turbo Coupe with substantial retail discounts by the second quarter of 1984, further exacerbating the SVO's value gap.

In 1986, Ford dealers were not generally part of the loop to receive product information and support for sales and promotion staff to reach the market Ford was hoping to tap. Brochures and other materials supplied with the models lacked the information necessary to promote and sell a car that could easily be dismissed as overpriced.

Eventually, executives at Ford realized what had happened. An internal document contained the following: "Insufficient retail sales capabilities in the area of prospecting and selling sophisticated cars. Dealers were not experienced in building and managing upscale traffic and did not recognize the need to place SVO units in demonstrator service. Sales personnel were deficient in product knowledge, in product demonstration skills, sports car prospecting methods, and in product-oriented selling techniques necessary to work successfully with the typical SVO prospect." Consequently, there were only 1,642 dealers who stocked and sold an SVO in the calendar year 1984, and fewer than 20 dealers sold more than 10 units for the year.

Visually, the SVO was just not different enough from other Mustangs to distinguish the car's unique technical attributes and support its higher price position. To many dealer sales personnel it was "just a Mustang for $16,000."

The price reductions of mid-1984 and during the beginning of 1985 severely impacted the value of used SVO models. This value disruption effectively shut out 1984 model buyers who wanted to move up to the more sophisticated 1985 1/2 model, but couldn't get a fair price for their trade-ins. This was unfortunate because the 1985 model was a better car and cost less, too.

And so it went. Eventually, Ford abandoned the SVO and continued with the more successful Mustang GT. Later a Ford executive said, "... as we learned in 1984, time and persistence is required to build retail sales capabilities in the area of sophisticated performance cars." It is a lesson that Ford learned very well.

1984–1986 Mustang SVO

The heart of the Mustang SVO was yet another version of the 2.3l four-cylinder engine. It was the same engine that the Ford Pinto used in 1971. Similar to the Turbo GT engine, this engine came with an intercooler and EFI to boost horsepower to 175. Maximum boost was 14 psi, and was electronically controlled. Other features included a revised front suspension with Koni adjustable shocks, 1.12 inch front anti-roll bar and .67 inch rear anti-roll bar, four wheel disc brakes, the Quadra-Shock rear suspension (with Koni shocks) from the Thunderbird Turbo Coupe, and 16x7 inch aluminum wheels with P225/50VR Goodyear NCT tires.

This is the 2.3l Turbo four cylinder used in the SVO. It put out over 200hp.

The SVO was equipped with articulated front seats with adjustable lumbar support, a leather-wrapped steering wheel, and a premium stereo system. Major options were air conditioning, power windows and locks, a cassette deck, flip-up open-air sun roof, and leather interior. Exterior colors were Black, Dark Charcoal Metallic, Silver Metallic, and Canyon Red. Externally, the SVO got a unique grille, functional hood scoop, wheel spats in front of the rear wheel well openings, and a large biplane rear spoiler. The axle ratio was 3.73:1 in the 8.8 inch rear end.

The SVO was updated as a mid-year model for 1985. It was changed visually through the use of flush headlamps, but the important changes were not visible. There were several changes to the engine, including a higher performance camshaft, a reworked intake manifold and turbocharger, a freer flowing split exhaust system, larger fuel injection nozzles (rated at 35 lb/hr instead of 30 lb/hr), and a one-pound increase in the turbo boost. These all resulted in an impressive rating of 205hp. The use of redesigned brackets made the engine far smoother as well. The suspension was made tighter with a 14.7:1 ratio steering. Teflon-lined stabilizer bar bushings contributed to improved handling, as did the Goodyear Eagle tires that replaced the NCT's.

In its final year of production, 1986, the SVO was essentially an extension of the 1985 1/2 production run. Horsepower was down, rated to 200hp, not due to any mechanical difference but as a result of the lower octane fuel that became common.

There was a DOHC (double overhead camshaft) 2.3 275hp engine made for the SVO, but it never made it beyond the prototype stage.

1987–93 MUSTANG OVERVIEW

The Mustang was in its ninth year of production before it received its first major restyle. Ford gave the Mustang a much needed facelift, emulating the aero-look of the company's other offerings. From the rear and side, the Mustang still looked the same, but the front definitely looked different.

The new GT achieved a totally different look with a redesigned nose sporting dual flush fitting head-

139

The Mustang made a slight styling change in 1987, and then for all intents and purposes stayed the same for seven years. This is the LX hatchback.

The LX became the model for those who did not prefer the aero package that came with the 1987 GT. Mechanically, both models were identical.

The Mustang GT got a new aero package for 1987. This look would stay with the Mustang until 1993.

The 5.0 liter Mustang V-8. It put out 225hp and was used in Mustang cars from 1987–1993.

Everyone thinks of the GTs when a 1979-93 Mustang is mentioned, but the everyday two door Mustang notchback outsold all others.

The fastest Mustang of the 1987–93 era is the two door notchback LX with the 5.0l engine. The reason is that this model is lighter than the other models, ergo faster.

Over 15,000 Police Specials were sold over the years. These were two door LX's powered with the 5.0 liter engine. There were very few cars that could outrun these Mustangs.

lights. A ground effect skirt package with scoops in front of each wheel opening extended around to the rear, which gave the car a much lower appearance. The C-pillar treatment achieved a sleeker look, too. The hatch retained the same rear wing, but added unique louvered rear tail lights.

For the next seven model years, the Mustang stayed the same. Amazingly it continued to sell well. During the last two years, 1992-93, the overall design started to appear a little tired, but the costs associated with the car had been amortized over an extended period. Ford concentrated on other projects and cars and basically took a ride on what was left of a good thing.

1990

About the only thing new about this Mustang was the addition of a driver's side airbag. After four years the car, for all intents and purposes, remained the same. Yet the Mustang was more popular than ever. A growing cottage industry had sprung up around the car, dealing in after-market new engine accessories and body parts, and just about anything else that could be considered Mustang-related. In the way that the first-generation Mustangs appealed to the baby-boomers, the third-generation Mustangs have captured the hearts of their children and grandkids.

1990 Limited Edition

A Limited Edition LX convertible was made available in 1990. It was available in Deep Emerald Jewel Green, with a white top and white leather interior with Sports Seats. On the exterior, the

1990 was the first year of the "Feature car," as it was called. These were limited production convertibles with a special paint scheme. The first were known as the 7-Up cars and were painted Deep Emerald Jewel Green.

Deep Jewel Green paint extended to the bodyside moldings and the dual remote outside mirrors. Like other Mustangs, the car had a rear decklid luggage rack.

Many people think of these cars as the 7-Up cars. The 7-Up Bottling Company had intended to give away 30 of these cars at the 1990 National Collegiate Athletic Association basketball finals. In an audience participation contest, anyone sinking a basket from center court with one try could drive home in one of the cars. The contest was cancelled at the last minute, but the name remains.

The car is also rumored to have been considered the 25th Anniversary car, but there's no substantial evidence of this.

It should be noted that the Deep Emerald Jewel Green paint was used in 1991 but the the dash pad and console were not white leather. Those cars had a gray dash pad and console instead, and the five-star (spoke) wheels.

A total of 4,103 cars were built: 1,360 five-speeds and 2,743 automatics. 261 were exported.

1991

The Mustang continued to be offered but with a few changes. Several options were added for 1991, including new 16x7 inch five-spoke aluminum wheels that made the car look better. They were easier to keep clean than the previous wheels, too. Sales were lower than the year before, and the Camaro, with 100,838 units, and the Firebird, with 50,454 units, did better than the Mustang.

Enthusiasts scratched their heads in wonder

Although the Mustang GT looked the same, it did get new 16 inch wheels in 1991. The 16x7 inch wheels gave the car a more modern look.

The 1992 Mustang GT from the rear.

The second feature car was known as the Summer Special. It was painted Vibrant Red, and it was the first convertible to have a rear spoiler.

because it definitely seemed as though Ford had forgotten about the car. It was now five years since the Mustang had received any major changes.

1992

1992½ Limited Edition

Also known as a Summer Special, this convertible was painted Vibrant Red with a white top, and was only available as an LX. Only one engine was available, the 5.0l V-8, with either a T-5 speed manual or the four-speed automatic.

Color-keyed side moldings, mirrors, door trim, and windshield frame were all part of the package. This Mustang was the first convertible to have a rear spoiler. It was made from blow-molded plastic and built by GE-Norel. In addition, the 1992½ Mustang had the five-spoke 16x7 wheels. The Superior Wheel Company (Kansas) prepared these wheels by applying baked-on opal pearlescent paint over silver.

The interior was special, too. It featured white leather seats with black piping, black carpet, white door panels, an ebony dash, and a black Lori cloth headliner. This was a first for Mustang, and instructions for attaching this headliner were included in a special sun visor sleeve.

A total of 2,019 units were built.

The last two feature cars were released in 1993. This is the Oxford White car.

The 1993 Canary Yellow feature car was the only one to be fitted with chrome wheels.

1993

This was another year where there were minimal changes made to the Mustang. Two models called Summer Specials made an appearance with new sound systems. That was it.

1993 LIMITED EDITION

They were painted the same way as the 1992½ Vibrant Red Summer Special, in Summer Special Canary Yellow and Oxford White. The Canary Yellow car also got chromed 16x7 five-spoke aluminum wheels. The engine available for both cars was the 5.0l V-8 with either a T-5 speed manual or the four-speed automatic.

Color-keyed side moldings, mirrors, door trim, and windshield frame were all part of the package. Like the 1992 1/2 Vibrant Red Summer Special Mustang, these Mustangs also included a rear spoiler. It was made from blow-molded plastic and it was built by GE-Norel. The headrests are embossed with galloping ponies and the floor mats have ponies to match.

The convertible top color was limited to white or black with the Canary Yellow or white with the Oxford White car.

There were a total of 1,500 Oxford White cars and 1,503 Canary Yellow cars built.

1993 COBRA

This is the street 1993 SVT Cobra. It was a no-nonsense car relying on solid engineering instead of ornamentation.

Starting in the Cobra Jet days, Ford had gotten into the habit of using the Cobra name on Mustang applications that were successively less powerful. It must have seemed like the right thing to do at the time, but the unfortunate and unintended result was the denigration of the Cobra name.

Understandably, there was trepidation on the part of enthusiasts with the introduction of the 1993 SVT Cobra. Everyone was wondering what the new Ford SVT group was really up to. Was it really possible for Ford to produce a Mustang worthy of the Cobra name and, just as important, could they continue to do so in the coming years?

In many ways, the 1993 Cobra was actually a stop-gap measure. Undoubtedly by 1993 the Fox platform was becoming out of date, as was the venerable 5.0l V-8. Still, there was enough life left in both the chassis and engine to hold off the newly redesigned Camaro and Firebird until the new 1994 Mustangs hit the dealerships.

Ford's SVT goal was to produce a Mustang that performed better than the current Mustang GT. The GT's strong point had always been acceleration. It was a traditional type of muscle car, with a strong grunt motor coupled to a fairly stiff suspension to ensure that all the power got to the ground. These elements were coupled with a strong visual package that reeked of high-performance.

The Cobra needed to have more power and better road manners than the current GT. It also required its own unique look. The result wasn't a perfect package by any means, but the SVT certainly accomplished its goals. It was an excellent first effort

Whereas the Mustang GT's styling blared high performance, the Cobra's styling was far more subtle. In front, the Cobra used the GT's lower grille which housed the foglamps, but dispensed with the GT's side scoops. The front fascia featured a grille opening (the GT's was closed) that featured a running horse emblem. A one-piece fascia with cutouts for the exhaust tips and a unique rear wing spoiler mounted on the hatch/deck-lid completed the rear.

The 5.0 liter SVT Cobra engine.

Cobra snake emblems replaced the 5.0 emblems. The snake's head pointed towards the front of the car on the driver's side, and towards the rear on the passenger side. The rear deck-lid had a Cobra emblem affixed on the left side.

The tail light bezels seemed familiar to the astute Mustang aficionado; in fact, they were the same units (modified to use the newer style bulbs) used on the SVO Mustangs.

The Cobra used the same interior as the Mustang GT. This included full instrumentation, articulated cloth/vinyl front sport seats with power lumbar support, premium electronic AM/FM cassette system with integrated clock and six speakers, power side view mirrors, power windows, power locks, and air conditioning with manual controls. The Cobra had white-faced instruments, and these have become a Cobra trademark. The Cobra also had specially embroidered floor mats.

There were actually few options available with the Cobra. The listed flip-open air roof became available only on Cobras produced after February 1, 1993, and the Super Sound System, listed on the sales brochure, was never released to the public.

In addition to the 1993 Cobras, Ford's SVT division built a small run of 107 Cobra R Mustangs designed for use in showroom stock racing. While mechanically similar to the standard Cobra, Cobra Rs were outfitted with a firmer suspension and were painted Vibrant Red. Unfortunately, several factors made it difficult for the R model to compete against GM's redesigned 1993 Firebird and Camaro. The Mustang's brakes, while adequate for street use, weren't up to the task on the track. In addition, the Mustang's small gas tank made for more frequent pit stops, and the 5.0l V-8 just didn't put out enough power. These problems were all addressed later on the 1995 version of the Cobra R.

However, the biggest problem the R models had was

The most powerful Mustang of the 1979–93 era was the 1993 Cobra. It was manufactured by a subsidiary of Ford called SVT (Special Vehicle Team). This is the Cobra R—a model that was supposed to be sold to racers but disappeared into private collections instead.

that few of them ever actually made it to the track. They were mostly bought up by collectors rather than racers, which was not what Ford had intended. Through circuitous means the cars were purchased by individuals with no intention of ever racing them.

A total of 4,993 street versions and 107 Cobra R models were built.

PROSPECTS

Other than the 1979 Pace cars, the 20th Anniversary Special, and the SVO, GT convertibles are the best bets for collectibles in the making. The 1985 and later versions with their distinctive styling and higher horsepower, however, may demonstrate a higher propensity for appreciation.

Regarding other four- and six-cylinder Mustangs, it is debatable whether they will ever achieve collector value.

12
1994–1998 Mustang

PRODUCTION

1994 Mustang

2dr coupe 3.8l	48,873
2dr convertible 3.8l	19,471
2dr coupe GT	35,137
2dr convertible GT	27,582
2dr Cobra coupe	5,009
2dr Cobra convertible	1,002
Total	137,074

1995

Base coupe	86,379
Base convertible	18,593
GT coupe	47,088
GT convertible	16,668
GTS coupe	6,370* (included in GT coupe)
Cobra coupe	4,255
Cobra convertible	1,003
Total	185,986

1996 Mustang

Base coupe	61,187
Base convertible	15,246
GT coupe	31,624
GT convertible	17,917
Cobra coupe	7,496
Cobra convertible	2,510
Total	135,620

1997 Mustang

Base coupe	56,812
Base convertible	11,606
GT coupe	18,464
GT convertible	11,413
Cobra coupe	6,961
Cobra convertible	3,088
Total	108,344

1998 Mustang

Base coupe	99,801
Base convertible	21,254
GT coupe	28,789
GT convertible	17,024
Cobra coupe	5,174
Cobra convertible	3,480
Total	175,522

1994

Imagine if the original 1965 Mustang had run, basically unchanged, for 15 model years. Would people have continued to buy Mustangs in the same numbers? Probably not, but that was the case during the 1980s. With minimal styling and mechanical changes, Ford was able to continue selling the same car in great enough numbers to make it profitable and still keep the Mustang mystique going. Alas, all good things must end and finally in 1994, the Mustang got a much-needed overhaul. Giving

This is a 1994 Mustang GT convertible. The horse came back in the front grille and that was important. The Mustang got a modern look, and there were mechanical improvements to the car as well. Still, it was a Fox underneath it all.

The 1994 Mustang GT from the back.

Ford a little more impetus to modernize the Mustang was the fact that GM's pony cars, the Camaro and Firebird, were restyled for the 1993 model year.

The most obvious change was in the styling. You might not say that the 1994 Mustang was all new, but the body (and interior) certainly were. Using the traditional long hood and short deck approach, the 1994 Mustang exhibited the currently fashionable wedge look which tended to make the car look slightly jacked-up sitting still. The side sculpturing definitely evoked the past, as did the rear triple-lens tail light treatment, and of course, the Mustang logo.

While the 1979–93 Mustangs were three-door hatchbacks, the 1994 became a two-door coupe. Besides the improved styling, getting rid of the hatch resulted in a stiffer, stronger platform. As before, a convertible was available.

Beneath its pretty new skin, the Mustang was basically a carryover of the Fox platform. It was definitely more rigid and stiffer; according to Ford, the coupe structure was fifty-six percent better in bending stiffness and forty-four percent better in torsion stiffness. The quest for additional stiffness resulted in a much improved convertible structure as well—sixty-five percent better bending and a noteworthy eighty percent increase in torsional stiffness. This resulted in a Mustang that was quieter, handled better, and inspired confidence.

The wheelbase was slightly longer (0.75 inch), while the track was 3.7 inches longer on the base model and 1.9 inches longer on the GT. Four-wheel disc brakes were standard, with an antilock braking system (ABS) optional.

The suspension, which features minor tweaks, was also a carryover, with McPherson struts in the front and a live axle in the rear. The quad rear shock arrangement was standard on the GT. One improvement was the use of a rear anti-roll bar on the base Mustang. Standard on the GT were P205/65R15s with 16x7.5 inch wheels with 17x8 inch wheels optional. The optional tires were P245/45ZR17s with 17x8 inch wheels.

The interior was redesigned as well on the 1994 Mustang. Dual air bags, a power driver's seat, and tilt-steering were standard equipment. The coupe featured a split-fold back seat. The last time Mustangs had a fold-down rear seat was in 1973.

Thankfully, the 2.3l four-cylinder engine was dropped on the 1994 car and replaced by the 3.8l V-6 as the standard Mustang engine. The V-6 had last been used in a Mustang in 1986. Unlike the 1986 version, the new V-6 had a tuned port injection system and tubular headers, which helped account for its 145hp output.

For the enthusiast, the tried-and-true 5.0l V-8 engine was the only one available for the GT. A nice motor, but its 215hp wasn't quite enough, at least when compared to the Camaro Z28 or Firebird Trans Am, which had 275hp on tap. As expected, Ford's 4.6l modular V-8 replaced the 5.0l in 1996.

Standard with both engines was the B&W T-5 five-speed manual transmission with the four-speed automatic AOD optional. Other improvements for the 1994 model included dual airbags, standard driver's power seat, optional ABS brakes, standard tilt wheel, and an optional hardtop for the GT convertible.

1994 Cobra

As the Mustang received the new body for 1994, the Cobra got its share of changes as well. In the front, the Cobra got its own front fascia with round fog lights and its own unique reflector head-lamps; the Mustang GT had come with rectangular fog lamps. Replacing the GT emblems were the Cobra snake emblems. The Cobra also got a different rear spoiler with a built-in LED stop lamp; the stop lamp on the GT was mounted on the deck lid. The Cobra was available in three colors: Rio Red Tinted Clearcoat, Crystal White, and Black Clearcoat.

The 5.0l V-8 engine was essentially carried over from the 1993 Cobra, but there were some minor differences. The engine for 1994 was rated at 240hp at 4,800 rpm, which is 5hp more than the 1993 version. The difference was attributed to a different calibration of the engine's management system. Torque output remained unchanged, but it came in at a higher rpm (4,000).

Cobra identification was used on the engine as follows: "Cobra" was cast onto the upper intake manifold; "Cobra" was embossed on the valve covers; and "Cobra" was stamped on the serpentine belt and on the lower radiator hose.

This is a 1994 Concept car that SVE built (Special Vehicle Engineering). It was powered by a Boss 429 engine that was enlarged to 608 cubic inches! Needless to say, that car was extremely fast.

The 1994 Cobra used the same upper and lower intake manifold as the 1993 model; the regular 1994 5.0l Mustang GT engine used a lower profile intake setup, which was the same one found on the Thunderbird. This was necessary because the 1994 Mustang had a lower hood. SVT chose to continue using the 1993 manifold because it produced more power; the tradeoff was the removal of the cowl-to-strut tower brace because of interference problems. The manifold featured larger diameter runners and also used a 60 mm throttle body and a 70 mm mass air meter. Replacing the stock 19 lb.hr. fuel injectors were 24 lb.hr. units. Adding to the engine's durability was the addition of an engine oil cooler.

The 1994–95 Cobra came with larger tires than the 1993 model. The tires were P255/45ZR17 Goodyear Eagle GS-Cs mounted on 17x8 inch cast aluminum alloy wheels. These tires were one size larger than the optional tires that could be ordered on the Mustang GT (P245/45/ZR17). The Cobra

The 1994 Boss from the rear.

The Boss 429 engine that was used in the 1994 Boss concept car. The intake system was a fabricated piece.

also got its own unique wheels and a 17 inch mini spare to replace the standard size mini spare. The five-speed transmission was carried over from 1993, as was the 8.8 inch rear axle and gear ratio.

The springs on the Cobra were softer than the GT's. The fronts were 400 lbs.in. linear rate springs, while the GT's were 400-505 lbs.in. variable rate units. The rear springs were linear rate units rated at 160 lbs.in. on the Cobra and 165-265 lbs.in. variable-rate units on the GT.

The front anti-sway bar on the Cobra measured 25 mm as compared to the larger 30 mm unit used on the GT; the rear bars measured 27mm on the Cobra and 24mm on the GT. All anti-sway bars on the 1994 Mustangs were tubular.

The Cobra was equipped with a four-wheel disc brake setup; the front discs measured 13.0 inches while the rears were 11.65 inches in diameter. An ABS was standard on the Cobra.

In the interior, the GT's 150 mph speedometer was replaced with a 160 mph unit and the shift knob, boot, and parking brake were leather-wrapped. Cobra badges replaced the Mustang running horse on the steering wheel airbag cover. The Cobra also got its own unique floor mats.

Options on the Cobra included a leather interior, remote keyless entry, and the Mach 460 stereo/CD system. These options were all standard equipment with the 1994 Pace car replica, too.

Other standard features included dual airbags, articulated sport seats with a four-way power driver's seat, a premium electronic AM/FM stereo cassette player, and the power equipment group, which included dual electric remote control mirrors, power side windows, power door locks, and a power deck lid release. Also standard was a rear window defroster, speed control, the Cobra floor mats, and dual illuminated visor mirrors.

1994 Pace Car

The 1994 Mustang was chosen to be the official Pace Car of the 1994 Indianapolis 500 race. Five Cobra convertibles were built for this purpose and prepped by Jack Roush for use on the track. Three were used on the track and the other two were used for display and parade functions. The other convertibles used at the track to shuffle VIPs around were actually Mustang GTs with the Pace Car decals.

The Pace car Cobras did not have the standard five-speed manual transmission; instead, they were fitted with Ford's four-speed AOD automatic. In addition, the cars were fitted with a roll bar, a 15

The 1994 Pace Car convertible. This example has the decals that signify it was a Pace Car convertible.

This is a 1994 Pace Car convertible, but without the side decals. All convertibles were painted red.

gallon fuel cell, a Halon fire extinguisher system, and the usual emergency lights. The Cobra I.D. label was not used on the Pace cars.

1,000 replicas were built for sale to the public. All were painted Rio Red and had a saddle leather interior. The convertible top was saddle as well. Besides the SVT certificate, each Pace car got its own sequentially numbered dash emblem, located in front of the shifter.

The Pace car decals were shipped in the trunk of each Cobra, giving each owner the option of putting them on or not. One minor difference between the decals used on the Pace cars used at the race and the replicas was the Indianapolis Motor Speedway logo. On the track cars, the wheel on the logo was white; on the replicas it was gray. Cobra identification was not used on the Pace car's valve covers either.

1995

The most significant addition to the Mustang lineup was the GTS model. It was basically a stripped down Mustang GT that was more affordable.

The GT's driveline, the 5.0l V-8, transmission, rear axle, and 16.5 inch wheels, were standard equipment on the GTS. Externally, the GTS did not have the GT's fog lamps or a rear spoiler. It did have "Mustang GT" embossed on the rear bumper cover and the Mustang GT fender emblems.

The GTS used the same interior as the base V-6 Mustang but did include the GT's instrument pod. Air conditioning, an AM/FM cassette player, power side mirrors, and a four-way power driver's seat were all standard equipment. All options that were available on the V-6–powered Mustangs were also available on the GTS.

Production for the GTS was between November 28, 1994, and August 11, 1995. A total of 6,370 units were built, divided up as follows: 4,848 with the five-speed manual, and 1,522 with the automatic.

GTS production by color is as follows:

Canary Yellow	344
Vibrant Red	25
Rio Red	777
Laser Red	1,123
Sapphire Blue	96
Bright Blue	197
Deep Forest Green	1,002
Teal	217
Opal Frost	312
Black	1,430
Crystal White	847

1995 SVT Cobra

Save for the different wheels, and the Modular engine in 1996, the Cobra's remained basically the same until the car got restyled for 1999. This is a 1995 model.

The 1995 Cobra was virtually unchanged from the 1994 version. The convertible became a regular production model and for 1995, all convertibles were painted black and all had a black leather interior.

Probably the most interesting and unique option on the 1995 Cobra convertible was the removable hardtop. Removing and replacing the top was a two man operation. The top came with its own carrier for holding the top when it wasn't installed on the car. The factory hardtop could not (easily) be retrofitted to other Mustang convertibles. The A pillar attachment point was different and there were rear defroster wiring differences as well. The top was

The last of the pushrod engines—the 1995 R model powered by a 351 c.i. V-8. Like the 1993 R model, the 1995 R model was more successful as a race car.

The 5.8l engine used in the 1995 R model.

originally supposed to be available on the 1994 Mustang convertible, but none had been produced. It was listed as an $1825 option.

500 were installed on 1995 Cobras; although it was supposed to be a Cobra-only option, several 1995 GTs were sold with the removable hardtop as well.

SVT built 250 Cobra R Mustangs for showroom stock racing in 1995. Unlike the previous 1993 R model, the 1995 R was equipped with Ford's 5.8l (351 c.i.) V-8 rated at 300hp with 365 lbs./ft. torque. As the Borg-Warner T5 manual transmission was not designed for so much torque, SVT used a stronger Tremec-made unit.

The suspension on the Cobra R model featured heavier front/rear springs with larger front/rear anti-sway bars and Koni shocks and struts. The Cobra R used the same PBR brakes that were standard on the street Cobra, with larger 17x9 inch wheels mounting P255/45ZR-17 B.F. Goodrich Comp T/A tires. The Cobra R was also equipped with a larger 20-gallon fuel cell (versus a 15.4 gallon gas tank on the stock Cobra) and a unique fiberglass hood. In keeping with its performance mission, the R did not have a rear seat, radio, air conditioning, power windows/locks/mirrors, sound insulation, or fog lights. The only color available was Crystal White.

In many ways, it was the last hurrah for the 351 c.i. and pushrod engines in general. The 351 c.i. engine first saw use in Mustangs in 1969, and actually, it was a derivative of the famous 289 c.i. V-

8. The 289 goes back to 1961, when the first incarnation of the engine, the 221 c.i., was introduced. When one considers the lead time required to bring a product to market, the engine had its roots well into the 1950's.

1996

This is a Cobra that uses the Mystic paint. The paint changes color as the sun and varying light moves over it. It was available in 1996 and in 2004.

Although the SN-95 (Fox) platform was carried over with minimal changes, there were significant changes under the hood.

The 5.0l V-8 was finally retired and replaced by a 4.6l version of the Ford's modular V-8. The most unique feature of the modular V-8 was its chain-driven single overhead camshaft (SOHC) design. The 4.6l features considerably improved porting over the old 5.0l and thus has better breathing potential. The engine used a 65 mm throttle body with an 80 mm mass air sensor. It was rated at 215hp at 4400 rpm with 285 ft.lb. torque at 3500 rpm. Besides the SOHC cylinder heads, the engine featured four-bolt main bearing caps for durability and a relatively square bore and stroke, 3.55x3.54 inches, for good low end torque.

Along with the new engine, the 1996 V-8 powered Mustang got a new transmission, the Borg-Warner T45 five-speed. The transmission, which weighed in at 110 pounds, had a torque rating of 320 ft.lbs. And unlike the T5, the bell housing was an integral part of the transmission casing, which makes for a more rigid structure.

The 8.8 inch rear axle was carried over from 1995 and used a 2.73:1 axle ratio. A 3.27:1 ratio was optional. The brakes on all Mustangs were upgraded to a four-wheel disc setup. The front discs measured 10.8 inches and the rear discs 10.5 inches. ABS was optional.

The GT's suspension was carried over for 1996. In the front, 400/505 lb.in. variable rate springs were used with a 30mm anti-sway bar. In the rear, 165-265 lb.in.

A 1996 Mustang GT.

variable rate springs with a rear anti-sway bar measuring 25mm were used. The rear bar for 1996 was 1mm larger than the one used in 1995.

Externally, all Mustangs received a new tail lamp treatment, featuring three vertical bars. Mustang GTs were also equipped with new GT 4.6l fender emblems.

1996 SVT Mustang Cobra

There were some subtle changes to the Cobra's styling for 1996. Most noticeable was the domed hood, necessary to clear the new 4.6l modular engine. The tail lamps were also redesigned, featuring three vertical bars, which were reminiscent of the first-generation Mustang tail lights. The rear spoiler was also changed, and COBRA lettering was stamped on the rear valance panel. Also new were 2.75 inch flared tailpipe outlets.

This shows the 1969-70 Boss 429 on the left, the 1996 DOHC modular V-8 in the center, and the 1965 427 SOHC on the right. The two older engines (429 and 427) were huge and exotic for their time but the modular easily joined their league. The modular fits in the Mustang's engine compartment with no trouble at all. Photo courtesy of Ford Motor Company

Because the new 4.6l modular engine was wider and taller than the 5.0l V-8, it necessitated changes to the Mustang's chassis. The No. 2 crossmember was modified to accommodate the engine's increased height and its oil pan, and the modification to the crossmember also resulted in improved structural rigidity. Also revised in this process was the front suspension's geometry. There was also a change in the power brake system for space reasons. A compact hydraulic system replaced the previous vacuum system.

The Cobra's rack and pinion system was also modified to use helical gears, and the previous plain bushings were replaced with roller type.

The Cobra continued to be equipped with 17x8 inch cast alloy wheels; these wheels were similar to the 1994-95 version but the wheel openings were painted a dark gray metallic color. Tires were changed to P245/45ZR-17 B.F. Goodrich Co. T/As. The tires were one size smaller than the Goodyear P255s used in 1995, but they were also one pound lighter each, which reduced unsprung weight.

The 1996 Cobra was equipped with the 1995 Mustang GT's higher rate springs and a thicker front anti-roll bar. The front springs were 400-505 lb.in. variable-rate units, and the rear springs were also variable-rate units rated at 165-265 lb.in. The front anti-sway bar on the Cobra measured 29 mm, while the rear bar remained unchanged at 27 mm.

The biggest change was the use of Ford's 4.6l modular V-8 engine for the Cobra. Even though it had the same bore and stroke (3.55x3.54 inch) as the 4.6l modular V-8 used in the Mustang GTs, the Cobra version featured an aluminum cylinder block cast at Teksid, an Italian company located in Carmagnola, Italy. The block used six bolts to retain each nodular iron main bearing cap. Four bolts go through the top of the cap into the cylinder block; two more bolts go through the side of the block into the cap, in the same way the old FE 427 c.i. engines or Chrysler's 426 Hemi were cross-bolted. The engine uses a forged steel crankshaft and hot-struck powder-sintered connecting rods.

The Cobra's cylinder heads have a chain-driven, double overhead camshaft configuration with four valves per cylinder. The fuel-injection system utilizes a dual 57mm throttle body and an 80mm mass air sensor. The 4.6l also has a built-in engine oil cooler. The water-to-oil cooler is mounted on the left side of the block, and it has the oil filter mounted on its end.

The engine was assembled at Ford's Romeo, Michigan, engine plant by 12 two-person teams. Each engine has a plate affixed on the right valve cover with the initials of the two assemblers who put that particular engine together. Output was 305hp at 5,800 rpm, with 300 ft.lb. torque at 4,800 rpm.

Along with a new engine, the 1996 Cobra got a new transmission, the Borg-Warner T45 five-speed. The transmission, which weighed in at 110 pounds, has a torque rating of 320 ft.lb. Unlike the T5, the bell housing is an integral part of the transmission casing. This makes for a more rigid structure.

Color selection consisted of Crystal White, Black Clearcoat, Laser Red Tinted, and the unusual Mystic paint. The Mystic paint exhibited four major metallic colors—green, amber, gold, and purple—and the visual effect varied depending on light intensity and the angle from which it was viewed.

1997

The 1997 Mustang line received minimal changes. Save for a slight change in the front upper grille opening, there wasn't any change to the Mustang. This opening ducted more air to the new

The modular engine is truly big. It is made from state-of-the-art materials only dreamt about in the 1960s.

Every modular Cobra engine was signed by the two-man team who built the engine. A sticker was placed on the right valve cover. In 1997, the engines were embossed with the same information.

cross-the-board Mustang cooling system. All models had a wider and taller radiator and a larger diameter fan.

1997 SVT Mustang Cobra

The 1997 Cobra was basically unchanged, save for the same slight change in the front upper grille opening. Exclusive to the Cobra was a new parallel-flow air conditioning condenser.

1998

Once again, changes were minimal to the Mustang line. The 4.6l received minor tweaks to produce 225hp. The optional leather interiors received a new pattern design.

Two new options appeared on the options list. The GT Sport Group included the 17-inch five-spoke aluminum wheels, hood, and wrap-around fender stripes, a leather-wrapped shift knob (for manual transmissions), and an engine oil cooler.

The V-6 Sport Appearance Group, available only on the base Mustang, included 16 inch cast aluminum wheels, the rear spoiler, a leather-wrapped steering wheel, and a lower bodyside accent stripe.

The 1998 SVT Cobra was fitted with look-alike 1995 Cobra R wheels. Nice!

The 1998 SVT Cobra from the rear.

The 1998 interior was spruced up. A new leather pattern was used, and a redesigned console. The clock pod on the instrument panel was removed, and the clock function was integrated into the radio display. A CD player became part of the standard premium sound system as well.

1998 SVT Mustang Cobra

The changes on the 1998 Cobra can be described as minimal, at best. Visually, the most noticeable change was the wheels. 1998 Cobras were equipped with five-spoke Cobra R look-alike alloys measuring 17x8 inches.

A new leather pattern was used and there was a new console. A CD player became part of the standard premium sound system as well for the Cobra.

PROSPECTS

Taking the 1994–98 cars as a group, there is one car that stands out—the 1994 Pace Car. This car is bound to appreciate in time, at a faster pace than other Mustangs because of its limited production, and it looks pretty good, too.

Right now, we seem to be going through a "bigger is better" way of thinking, so it's likely that the 1996-up SVT Mustang Cobra, with the 4.6l modular engine, will see some appreciation. On the other hand, later Cobras (and Mustang GTs) have even more power than 1994-98 models. This makes the later cars with their bigger engines more desirable at the expense of the earlier cars. That is progress.

However, don't overlook the 1995 R model. With only 250 made and only with the 351 c.i. engine, it is definitely a collectible in the making. It is as close to a race car as a car can be and still be sold as a street car.

13
1999–2004 Mustang

PRODUCTION

1999 Mustang

Base coupe	73,180
Base convertible	19,299
GT coupe	19,634
GT convertible	13,699
Cobra coupe	4,040
Cobra convertible	4,055
Total	133,637
35th Anniversary Special	4,628

2000 Mustang

Base coupe	121,026
Base convertible	41,368
GT coupe	32,321
GT convertible	20,224
Cobra coupe	300
Cobra convertible	100
Total	215,383

2001 Mustang

Base coupe	75,321
Base convertible	30,399
GT coupe	32,511
GT convertible	18,336
Cobra coupe	3,867
Cobra convertible	3,384
Total	163,818

2002 Mustang

Base coupe	67,090
Base convertible	24,747
GT coupe	33,093
GT convertible	17,717
Cobra coupe	1,830*
Cobra convertible	1,041*
Total	145,518

*2002 production numbers include 2,772 early production 2003 Cobras built before the actual Mustang 2003 Job #1

2003 Mustang

Base coupe	59,943
Base convertible	26,500
GT coupe	26,955
GT convertible	17,135
Mach 1	9,652
Cobra coupe	6,600
Cobra convertible	4,110
Total	150,895

2004 Mustang

Mustang	124,532
Mach 1	7,182
Cobra coupe	3,768

Cobra convertible	1,896
40th Anniversary Special	4,529
Total	141,907

1999

This Mustang was extensively restyled, and the result was both evolutionary and gratifying. Definitive creases and lines that were angular replaced the smooth rounded lines of the 1994–1998 models. The side sculpturing became larger, leading to a taller rear side scoop. The object was to emulate the look of the first-generation Mustangs while maintaining a contemporary 1990s look. The only thing that didn't change from the 1994–98 models was the roof. Overall, the Mustang became slightly longer and wider.

The redesigned 1999 Mustang. It was an evolutionary change—it looked like the energized 1994–98 Mustangs.

The GT hood incorporated a simulated hood scoop and had larger, three inch exhaust tip extensions. The extensions measured 2.75 inches previously. All 1999 Mustangs also had a 35th Anniversary version of the tri-color emblem on the sides of the front fenders. Although not readily apparent, the rear decklid on all 1999 Mustangs was made from sheet molded compound to reduce weight and eliminate the possibility of corrosion.

The original Fox platform dating back to 1979 was used but with considerable refinements and improvements made to the 1999 Mustang's chassis. The revised floor pan sealing was retained, and the addition of foam in the rocker panels reduced road noise. Transmission and sub-frame connectors on the convertible also reduced, as Ford put it, "mid-car shake." A 1.5 inch increase in the drive tunnel height at the rear axle resulted in more rear suspension travel. In the interior, there were new fabrics and patterns, and a one-inch increase in seat travel for the driver's seat.

The 4.6l modular SOHC V-8 was rated at 260hp at 5,250 rpm with 300 ft.lb. torque at 4,000 rpm. This was achieved through the use of higher lift and longer duration camshafts, coil-on-plug ignition, bigger valves, and a revised intake manifold that increased intake flow above 2,000 rpm.

The Mustang GT also came with a modular engine but it wasn't the same as the Cobra version. It was a single overhead camshaft (SOHC) design with a 2 valve cylinder head.

Although the five-speed manual transmission was the same T45 used in previous years, for 1999 it was manufactured under license from Borg-Warner, by Tremec. Both the V-6 and V-8 Mustangs were equipped with a 3.27:1 rear axle ratio for 1999. New for the Mustang was an all-speed Traction Control System (TCS). The system was designed to control wheel spin under adverse road conditions.

A special 35th Anniversary Limited Edition Package was also available for the 1999 GT. It included 17 inch wheels, black appliqué trim, a black tape treatment on the hood, and a special black and silver interior. A total of 4,628 Mustangs were produced with this package.

1999 SVT Mustang Cobra

The 1999 SVT included all the styling changes common to other Mustangs, but also included round fog lights in the lower front fascia and a regular hood, whereas the GT used a hood that incorporated a simulated hood scoop. Both the Cobra and GT had three inch exhaust tip extensions.

One difference between the GT and the Cobra was that the grille running horse emblem wasn't surrounded by a chrome band. Cobras also did not have the 35th anniversary tri-color bar emblem on the sides of the front fenders.

The 4.6l DOHC modular V-8 remained the Cobra's sole powerplant. The engine, however, put out 15hp and 17 ft. lb. torque more than the 1998 version. This was due to different intake port geometry and a redesigned combustion chamber.

The 1999 ignition system was changed to a coil-on-plug system, again to aid the combustion process. A better type of knock sensor, a differential linear type, replaced the former resonant knock sensor to better control any impending detonation.

There were also major changes in the Cobra's drivetrain. The transmission, rear axle, and ratio were a carryover from the 1998 Cobra; the differential case, though, was aluminum. The transmission was again the T45 five-speed manual found on 1998 models, like the Mustang manufactured by

Tremec, under license from Borg-Warner for 1999. Tremec-built T45s have the word "Tremec" cast into the housing.

The most significant change on the Cobra, though, was the use of a new independent rear suspension system (IRS). The system used short and long arms mounted on a tubular subframe with aluminum lower arms and upper arms made of steel. The subframe also held the aluminum differential case, which was borrowed from the Lincoln Mark VIII. The independent rear was mounted at the very same four mounting points that the regular Mustang solid-axle suspension utilized. Although the whole IRS setup weighed 80 pounds more than a comparable straight axle rear, there was a 125 pound decrease in unsprung weight with the IRS. The result was a better ride and better handling.

The independent rear design allowed for much stiffer rear springs, and the Cobra used 470 lb.in. springs along with a 26 mm tubular anti-roll bar. The Mustang GT used 210 lb.in. springs with a 23 mm solid bar.

The front suspension configuration remained unchanged but the position of the front struts was changed. The front spring rate was increased to 500 lb.in. (versus 450 lb.in. on the base and GT). The front anti-roll bar diameter was 28 mm.

Although the Cobra was supposed to be making 15hp more, several enthusiast magazines reported that the 1999 Cobra seemed slower than previous models. Several Cobra owners had their cars dyno tested and the engine was down on power.

On August 6, 1999, Ford stopped the sale of any unsold Cobras sitting on the dealer's lots and recalled the rest to replace the intake manifold, the engine management computer, and the entire exhaust system from the catalytic converters back.

This sort of thing doesn't happen very often in the car business, having a whole production run recalled. It shows that Ford did care about the Cobra and its customers, but it doesn't speak well of the car.

2000 SVT MUSTANG COBRA R

This Mustang was released with tremendous fanfare, even though it listed at $54,995. The R model certainly offered a lot of performance but at a very serious price. Still, with only 300 built, the low production numbers promised high resale values. No one expected that a serious challenge to this would appear from within Ford's own stable but it did.

The ultimate Mustang, at least in our opinion. The 2000 R model packs a mean wallop.

No other Mustang has a rear spoiler like the 2000 R model.

The 2003–04 SVT Mustang Cobra had more horsepower and cost $20,000 less that the 2000 R model, but the 2000 R model was unique enough to warrant a second look.

Following the pattern set by the 1993 and 1995 R model versions that preceded it, the 2000 model was not equipped with any luxury options such as air conditioning, stereo, power windows, rear seats, and power door locks. The standard seats were replaced with special Recaro versions which also incorporated a Cobra snake and R emblem on the headrest area. The snake and R emblem was also used on the reverse indicator letter on the transmission shifter.

The 2000 R model also has a modular engine. This one is a 2 valve SOHC design. It puts out 385hp.

The engine used on the Cobra was a specially modified version of Ford's 5.4l SOHC V-8 mated to a six-speed manual transmission. Output was 385hp at 6,250 rpm, with torque at 385 ft.lb. at 4,250 rpm. All R models were painted red.

Visually, the R model was distinguished by the tall rear wing spoiler and a front air dam. The low front air dam, with limited ground clearance, was easily removable for street use.

In our opinion, the 2000 Cobra R is probably the best and fastest Mustang made, and this includes the 2003-04 supercharged cars. While the supercharged cars may be just as fast in a straight line, there is nothing like the driving experience that the 2000 R can give.

Production was limited to 300 units. This has remained a very rare car! The acceleration and the handling make driving it feel like you're in a real race car. If you are into pure speed, then the 2000 R is definitely for you.

2000–2004 MUSTANG

Although it might be difficult to tell, the word "Cobra" is embossed on the rear bumper. Previously, the word "Mustang" had been used.

Changes to the 2000–2004 model Mustangs were minimal. They involved new exterior colors, sound systems, and so on, and the addition of a few new models.

One production change made during the 2004 model year was the addition of a new V-6. This was a 3.9l V-6 that replaced the previous 3.8l V-6. It did not offer an increase in power, weight, or fuel efficiency, however.

2001 Bullitt Edition Mustang

Introduced after the regular Mustang release in 2001, a special Bullitt edition was offered on the GT line. The original Bullitt Mustang was a special 1968 Mustang that actor Steve McQueen used in the film "Bullitt." The 2001 Bullitt Mustang got rocker panels with the word "Bullitt" embossed on them, special wheels, individual exterior and interior identification, its own pedals, shifter, 150mph speedometer, unique brake calipers, underhood clearcoat paint, and serialized special edition iden-

Following the pattern set years ago (during the 1990–93 era) Specials were introduced to make a lackluster model year appear to have new offerings. The first was the 2001 Bullitt Mustang, named after the 1968 movie by the same name. Photo courtesy of Ford Motor Company

The Bullitt Mustang interior. Photo courtesy of Ford Motor Company

The 2001 SVT Cobra came back after missing the 2000 model year. The 1999 models were recalled because the engines didn't put out the specified horsepower.

tification. The regular 260hp engine was massaged to get 5hp more out of it: 265hp with 315 ft.lbs. torque. It was only available with the manual shifter.

2003½ Mustang Mach 1

The 2003 Mustang Mach 1.

A new Mach 1 was also introduced in 2003. Since it had sold well 30 years ago, it was expected to give the tired Mustang brand an added boost, and it did.

The most visually arresting design cue on the 2003 Mach 1 was the retro Shaker scoop. The Shaker had originally been introduced on the 1969 Mach 1. The scoop had been designed to channel fresh air to the intake, thus increasing the breathing for improved power and torque. The scoop and the center powerdome hood were finished in low-gloss black.

The Mach 1 C-pillars feature a unique trim appliqué that gives the roofline a subtle retro look. To enhance the low-to-the-ground appearance, the car featured another classic Mach 1 trait, an air dam extension, painted low-gloss black. A low-gloss black stripe runs the length of the side just above the rocker moldings.

The seats have increased lateral support and are trimmed in one-of-a-kind comfort weave black leather that is reminiscent, of course, of the material that was unique to the original Mach 1.

There were other special features on the Mach 1, as well. The center stack and shifter bezel were painted in a gray accent finish and highlighted by an aluminum shift boot ring and aluminum shifter ball. The accelerator, brake, clutch, and dead pedals are polished aluminum. The gray-backed instrument cluster features unique retro-look dials.

One of the exciting things about the 1969–70 Mach 1 was the Shaker hood scoop. The 2003 Mach 1 also got the Shaker scoop.

The Mach 1 was powered by a 4.6-liter, 32-valve, dual-overhead cam V-8. The engine made use of specially calibrated cams, a modified upper intake to accommodate the Ram-Air system, a forged crank (cast crank in automatic transmission application), and performance exhaust manifolds to produce 310hp (308hp automatic).

The total Mach 1 production by color is as follows:

Black	1,611
Dark Shadow Gray	1,595
Zinc Yellow	869
Azure Blue	2,250
Torch Red	2,513
Oxford White	814
Total	9,652

2003 Ford 100th Anniversary Mustang

Ford's 100th year in business celebration presented a great opportunity to offer a special Mustang, so the Centennial Package was introduced in 2003.

The 100th Anniversary models were all black, and included Premium Verona-grain Imola leather seating surfaces in two-tone parchment. They also included the GT premium package, with 17 inch wheels, anti-lock brakes, and traction control; dual exhaust; power driver's seat with power lumbar support; leather-wrapped steering wheel; and Mach 460 AM/FM stereo with six-disc CD changer. The cars also had 100th Anniversary badges on the fender and decklid, and embossed on the seats.

2004 40th Anniversary Mustang

The 40th Anniversary Mustang GT. Photo courtesy of Ford Motor Company

Not to be left behind, the 40th anniversary of the introduction of the Mustang model was celebrated with a new offering as well. Every 2004 Mustang had a 40th Anniversary badge on the front fender. To make the model stand out, it was fitted with Arizona Beige Metallic performance stripes on the hood, lower rocker panels, and decklid, complemented by upgraded wheels (16 inches for the V-6 and 17 inches Bullitt wheels for the GT) with a special Arizona Beige Metallic accent.

The special 40th Anniversary models were available in Crimson Red, Black, or Oxford White, with a Medium Parchment interior. There was also a special interior for this model.

2003–2004 SVT Mustang Cobra

The big news for 2003, and probably for the entire Mustang line, turned out to be the supercharged V-8 engine. The Mustang Cobra's 4.6-liter DOHC V-8 was equipped with an Eaton™ supercharger and new aluminum alloy cylinder heads that produced 390hp at 6,000 rpm and 390 ft.lb. of torque at 3,500 rpm. The engine, using a cast-iron block, used special Manley forged H-beam connecting

One way to tell the 2003–04 SVT Cobra from the 2001 model was the larger bottom grille opening. The supercharged engine really makes horsepower.

All 2003–04 SVT Cobras came with a five-speed transmission. Good for some people, but not for everyone.

rods, forged pistons similar to those in the SVT F-150 Lightning, and an aluminum flywheel similar to the 2000 SVT Mustang Cobra R. The engine was mated to a TTC T-56 six-speed manual transmission. No automatic transmission was available.

Exterior design changes were used to distinguish the SVT Mustang Cobra from the regular production Mustang GT. While it retained the SVT-signature round fog lamps, the front fascia developed a more aggressive look. The hood was also redesigned, with the acquisition of flow-through scoops to help vent hot air from the engine compartment. Both the hood and rear deck were made of lightweight composite materials.

With the Supercharger, the 4.6l engine was rated at 390hp by Ford. It was actually around 420hp but Ford wanted to play it safe and not overrate it, as it had with the 1999 version. Photo courtesy of Brad Bowling

At the sides, the rocker panels were reshaped to simple, clean vertical surfaces. Color-keyed, fold-away outside mirrors were also unique to the Cobra, while the side scoops had new, horizontal fins to match those in the hood scoops. The rear deck lid featured an integrated spoiler with an LED center high-mounted stop lamp.

This is a 2004 SVT Cobra with the Mystic paint package. Unlike the previous use of this paint (1996), the interior got the same treatment as well. Photo courtesy of Ford Motor Company

The 2003 SVT Cobra joins the 2000 Cobra R as the only Mustangs ever factory-equipped with a six-speed gearbox: the TTC T-56. A new aluminum drive shaft with upgraded universal joints, a 3.55:1 gear set in the differential, and higher capacity half-shafts completed the changes to the 2003 powertrain.

Clearly, this was the fastest production Mustang to date, although saying so might elicit an argument from owners of the 2000 R model. The media agreed and gave the 2003 SVT superior ratings.

2004

There's not much to say about the 2004 model. The Cobra got some new colors, and a limited number (993) of SVT Mustang Cobra coupes and convertibles were available with the new Mystichrome Appearance Package.

The Mystichrome Package had shifting paint that moved the exterior color from green, to blue, to purple, and to black. The steering wheel and leather seats have also the same color-shifting properties.

2003 10th Anniversary SVT Cobra

Ten years after SVT introduced its first product—the 1993 SVT Cobra R—they released a special 10th Anniversary 2003 SVT Cobra.

The 10th Anniversary Package was available as either a coupe or convertible, and featured unique 17x9 inch dark argent painted anniversary wheels, red leather seating surfaces in the front and rear, interior trim with the appearance of carbon fiber, red painted brake calipers, and SVT 10th Anniversary badges on the floor mats and rear decklid. SVT produced 2,003 units of the Anniversary model; they were available in Torch Red, Black Clearcoat, and Silver Metallic.

PROSPECTS

Rating these models at this point may be a bit premature. When you compare the quality and quantity factors, the 2000 R Model may be the rarest of all 1999–2004 Mustangs. It can also safely be considered the most valuable as well. The supercharged 2003–04 SVT Mustang Cobras follow, with the Mustang GTs bringing up the rear.

With the exception of the 2000 R Model, all of these Mustangs are still in a downward cycle. Don't expect significant appreciation for now.

14
2005–2006 Mustang

The 2005 Mustang combined the styling of the 1969 Mustang along with engineering that really excels. The result is probably the best Mustang yet. Photo courtesy of Ford Motor Company

The last Mustangs I owned were a 1968 Shelby convertible and a 1969 Boss 429. Perhaps I am biased, but those models—well, they looked good and were exciting to own and to drive. Since then, I've never thought about owning a Mustang again. Yes, there have been some nice models here and there since but nothing to compare to my stallions. That is, until now.

Finally, with the 2005 models, Ford has shown that it still knows how to build fun cars. These Mustangs are exciting to drive and handle like cars that cost much more. They sound, feel, and drive like the real thing, and look the part too!

The 2005 Mustangs show their origins are firmly grounded in the models designed back in the 1960s. The long hood and short rear deck, the side C-scoops, the three-element tail lamps and galloping horse badge at the center of the grille are all authentic classic Mustang styling cues. The Mustang's shark-like nose imparts a predator attitude not seen since 1969, yet the jeweled, round headlamps in trapezoidal housings are a striking new and modern departure that works, and works very well. The car's aggressive stance gives it visual forward motion too. The 1969 Mustang has always represented a high water mark in design and performance, and so does the 2005, of which it is virtually a carbon copy. The 2005 Mustang is available as either a coupe or a convertible.

177

The grille is what does the most for the Mustang. Mean! Photo courtesy of Ford Motor Company

The 2005 Mustang GT looks right at home with other Mustangs and Ford performance cars. Photo courtesy of Ford Motor Company

This base Mustang doesn't have the grille lights or big wheels/tires. Still, it looks good! Photo courtesy of Ford Motor Company

This is the three-valve SOHC 4.6l that powers the 2005-06 Mustang GT. It puts out 300hp. Photo courtesy of Ford Motor Company

The 2005 Mustang is available in two distinct models. The base model is powered by a 4.0l V-6 that puts out 210hp at 5,250 rpm with 240 ft.lb. torque at 3,500, while the GT is powered by a 4.6l three-valve SOHC that pumps out 300hp at 5,750 rpm with 320 ft.lb. torque at 4,500 rpm. The GT can hit 0-60 mph at 5.2 seconds and the quarter mile time is in the low 13s.

A five-speed manual transmission has been standard on both engines but in 2005, a five-speed automatic also became available. The V-8 powered GT is equipped with the Tremec 3650 gearbox, while the V-6 uses the Tremec T-5. At the front suspension, MacPherson struts with reverse L lower control arms are used, while the solid rear uses a Panhard rod and an anti-roll bar. Ford engineers did an excellent job with the rear end, as the car handles beautifully. This was accomplished through the use of a 107.1 inch wheel base, which is almost six inches longer than the previous 1994–2004 models.

The standard four-wheel disc brakes have the biggest rotors and stiffest calipers ever fitted to a mainstream Mustang. Twin-piston aluminum calipers clamp down on 12.4 inch ventilated front brake discs on GT models. In the rear, the brake rotors are 11.8 inches in diameter, more than twelve percent larger than on the 2004 model. A four-channel antilock braking system (ABS) with traction control is optional.

In the interior, all Mustangs have a color-configurable instrument panel that lets the driver choose from more than 125 different color backgrounds, an industry first.

For 2006, a V-6 Pony package has become available. It includes a customized grille with GT-style round fog lamps and a chrome bezel or corral around the traditional Mustang prancing horse. It also includes an upgraded suspension featuring a larger front stabilizer bar, the addition of a rear stabilizer bar, and P235/55ZR17 tires on painted cast-aluminum wheels. These are the largest wheels and tires ever fitted to a V-6 Mustang. In addition, there are pony fender badges, lower door tape stripes, a rear spoiler, and the ABS.

The interior was completely redone for the 2005-6 Mustang. Photo courtesy of Ford Motor Company

The GTs offer four distinct wheel and tire combinations, including two 18 inch wheel packages. These are the largest wheels on a production Mustang. The 2000 R model got 18 inch wheels too, but it isn't considered a production model.

For 2006, the Mustang with the Pony package got this front grille, which emulates the GT. This package also includes larger wheels and tires. Photo courtesy of Ford Motor Company

The 2006 Mustang will include a Pony package that offers V-6 buyers larger wheels and tires, ABS, and a custom grille with fog lamps, much like the 1965 GT grille. The package will also include special pony emblems.

15
Basic Mustang Restoration

To bring this 1969 Boss 429 to this condition takes lots of time and money. For many, the joy of owning a collector car is in bringing out that diamond in the rough, and it's even nicer when the car also happens to be valuable.

When it comes to the actual nitty-gritty work of restoring a classic Mustang, some enthusiasts may prefer to hire out some or all of the restoration work. Although, part of the enjoyment of owning a collector car is working on it yourself, it's best not to overestimate your abilities or underestimate the time, money, and expertise required to restore one. The decision will have to rest upon your knowledge base and resources. A rusted-out car in need of major bodywork might be better off farmed out to a professional who will have the tools and resources to do a really good job. A well-maintained Mustang that has been protected from the elements and driven with care is a different story. Many enthusiasts see their restoration efforts as bringing a diamond out of the rough, but it's best to know your limits. Do thorough research, ask a lot of questions, and check the answers with more than one source. Despite the potential headaches the process of restoring a Mustang can be pleasurable and rewarding.

ORIGINAL VERSUS MODIFIED

The first requirement is to know exactly what the term "restoration" means: It is the process of returning an automobile to the exact condition it was in when it first left the assembly line. Anything less is not a restoration. Many classic era cars are refurbished, rebuilt, or renovated, but not restored. Altering a classic or antique car in any way renders it as modified. Modifications can take the form of improvements to the car's performance or to its appearance. For example, a modification can be the update of the ignition system through the use of an electronic ignition conversion kit. Electronic ignition is much more reliable than the conventional points ignition that most pre-1975 Mustangs have. Some enthusiasts also like the look of customized bodywork and paint on their cars, something that is definitely beyond the realm of originality.

POINTS TO CONSIDER

Understanding the rules before you play the game is essential. Concours competitions require strict originality, down to every original nut and bolt. This can be quite an expensive proposition because it requires a complete teardown and restoration of the car from the ground up. Obtaining an original owner's manual, researching parts and option codes, and utilizing new technologies like spectrometry analysis for original paint duplication are a necessity here. Scavenging for engine parts, drivetrains, original floor mats, dashboard knobs, door locks, and so on, can be fun, frustrating, and hugely expensive by turns. We know of deeply committed owner/restorers who have chartered small aircraft in pursuit of original trannies, belts, decals, steering wheels, and other "must haves" for concours designation.

A ground-up or body-off restoration means disassembling the entire car and reconditioning, rebuilding, and/or replacing all parts. With many older cars, a ground-up restoration entails lifting the body off the frame, as shown here. In unibody cars, which is what all Mustangs are, the suspension and engine are bolted directly to the body instead of to a separate frame.

It is also common for concours-level competition cars to sport clear plastic bags over the tires when they are moved from the travel trailer to the show-car lineup to preclude any possibility of soiling or wear on the tires or undercarriage. These cars are babied and protected in the extreme by owners who have paid for re-chroming, prime condition original tires, and sealers. Even sparkplug wires must conform to original specs.

Carlisle Events, located in Carlisle, PA, hosts numerous events for car and motorcycle enthusiasts and collectors. They hold spring and fall swap meets, plus car shows are held during the summer. www.carsatcarlisle.com.

This enthusiast decided to do some of the body work himself. It is entirely possible for an amateur to bring the car's bodywork to this stage prior to painting. By doing so, he'll save considerably.

For those interested in owning and driving their Mustang for fun, non-stock aftermarket parts abound to upgrade and improve your car's handling and braking. You can also end up with a very beautiful and respectable restoration using aftermarket parts manufactured to look like the real thing.

SAVE ORIGINAL PARTS

Remember to save all original parts you replace if you decide to modify your collector car. Also, try to make the modifications easily convertible. Thus, if you decide to install a different set of wheels, keep the old ones. The same applies if you install a larger carburetor, or update the ignition. Should you decide to sell the car at some point, it will be easier to attract buyers because the demand for original cars is greater than for those that are modified. Avoid engine swaps and body modifications. Such modifications are more difficult to reconvert to stock later on.

CONSIDER THE COSTS

Give some serious consideration to how much a Mustang restoration could cost. It's easy to get in over your head in the heated rush of buying and tearing down the car. Set a realistic budget and a timetable you can work within. Be prepared to exceed both the budget and timetable, because restorations rarely meet initial projections. One important consideration is whether the expense can be justified in terms of added value to the car. For example, will it make sense to invest $15,000 to restore a 1967 six-cylinder Mustang that is only worth $5,000? Of course, there are lots of other good reasons why someone would want to make such an investment, but dramatically increased market value shouldn't be one of them.

PLANNING AND PREPARATION

The first step in any restoration will have to be planning and preparation. It will ultimately save you time and money. It is essential that you spend time planning your restoration, from beginning to end, preferably on paper. Make a flow chart of areas to be worked on, tools and parts that need to be on hand or purchased, work to be farmed out, and work you intend to do yourself. Close attention to these details can make all the difference between a fun, pleasurable experience and a veritable nightmare that seems to have no end.

LOCATION

Brain surgery isn't performed on kitchen tables, and correct restorations can't be performed in driveways. You need to have a facility to store your project and all the parts and tools you need, and a place to work. Even if you're not going to restore the car yourself, a garage is still necessary; otherwise, the car will continue to deteriorate through exposure to the elements. The most basic garage must also be well lit, have enough working space for parts and tools and if at all possible, it should be heated. It's not much fun working on a car when it's only 25 degrees outside. Regarding space, you need at least a two-car garage with plenty of bench space to disassemble, restore, and reassemble components, room to paint, and lots of storage space for parts. And let's not forget ventilation. You want to make it to the end of the restoration and enjoy your car with your cognitive function intact.

Along with sufficient space, you'll need plenty of 110- and 220-volt outlets and heavy duty grounded electrical extensions. Overhead lamps are a necessity, and the walls should be painted white so your work area is bright. Also handy but not essential are running water and a large utility sink to clean parts in. Avoid cleaning engine parts with solvents in enclosed areas at all costs. This is very dangerous. Keep solvents away from water heaters. These cautions might seem over the top but people get hurt every year because they don't follow them.

TOOLS

The Eastwood Company has a variety of power and specialty tools, along with basic tools. Contact www.east woodco.com.

You can never have enough tools. At the very minimum you will need a complete set of hand tools. The set should include ¼, ⅜ and ½ inch drive socket sets with several ratchets, extensions, and the like, and a breaker-bar. If you're planning to assemble your engine, you'll also need a torque wrench, and an engine hoist might not be a bad idea either. Naturally, a good selection of screwdrivers, pliers, and vise-grips will be mandatory, and you'll also need specialized tools if you're planning to work on the brakes and suspension.

Despite access to a good selection of tools, there will be times when you'll find yourself going to the hardware or auto-parts store to get a special socket or tool because you just can't get to a bolt with what you have. There will also be tools or equipment you'll only need to use once or twice. Renting instead of buying these tools will help you stretch your budget. Work on components such as carburetors will require specialized tools as well. For example, some Holley Carburetors require a special type of screwdriver to remove the carburetor's metering plates. To work on the electrical system, a test light, voltmeter, and ohm meter will be necessary.

POWER TOOLS

Beyond hand tools, a compressor can be a handy piece of equipment. Pulling a 40-year-old car apart with hand tools takes time and effort. Parts meant to turn might be frozen, nuts and bolts might be stripped, and corrosion might make the teardown tedious and frustrating. Air tools cut your work time in half. A compressor is also useful for cleaning parts, and a necessity if you're going to do any painting. For disassembly and restoration work, if your budget allows, consider a sandblaster and a small glass-beader. A sandblaster can strip rust and debris from cast parts such as exhaust manifolds, and a glass-beader is a useful tool for cleaning rubber, aluminum, and metal parts without altering the surface texture. It beats trying to clean parts with a wire brush in a pail of mineral spirits.

To use a sandblaster, make sure your compressor is at least 2.5hp with a 20-gallon tank. Also, install a water separator to keep the air line to the sandblaster nozzle dry. Wet sand can't cut rust and paint. Refer to Appendix 3, "Mustang Sources," for sources of equipment, aftermarket parts, and restoration resources. If you decide to add equipment like this to your garage, you'll find The Eastwood Company (www.eastwoodco.com) to be a great source of supply. Call them to get their free catalog.

REFERENCE MATERIAL

A proper restoration is unlikely without access to good reference materials. A factory service manual provides the correct specs, illustrates the proper methods to disassemble and assemble parts, and usually includes useful drawings and photos. *Hemmings Motor News* (www.hemmings.com) is a good resource for vendors who specialize in manuals. Look under the "Books and Literature" section. Like everything else, it pays to shop around. Refer to Appendix 3 for suggestions. *Mustang 1964½–1973 Restoration Guide* is an excellent source of information; you can get it at Motorbooks International (www.motorbooks.com).

This magazine is a staple for the automotive world and you definitely need it. Hemmings publishes a monthly magazine, "Hemmings Motor News," which consists of classified ads but also has ads for other automotive-related items. Its web site is www.hemmings.com.

This is an ad for Mustangs Unlimited from "Hemmings." In it Mustangs Unlimited advertises some of their Mustang items. Quite an array of Mustang parts. www.mustangsunlimited .com

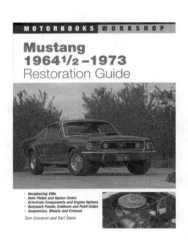

Probably the best compilation of Mustang factory service literature is the "Mustang 1964½–1973 Restoration Guide," by Tom Corcoran and Earl Davis. It is packed with 448 pages of information. Of course, if you wanted a factory publication, not only would it be expensive but it would also be considerably longer, for just one year!

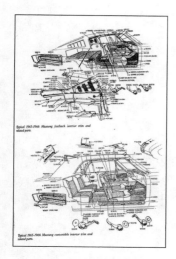

This page shows what the "Mustang 1964½–1973 Restoration Guide" consists of.

Reference manuals specific to your Mustang are a must. Some of these may be found in "Hemmings" or at some large flea market, such as the Carlisle Events held in Carlisle, PA. www.hemmings.com and www.carsat carlisle.com

PARTS

A full-blown restoration is going to call for a lot of parts to replace broken, worn-out, or missing parts. Where you locate and purchase them is dependent to a certain extent on how exact you want your restoration to be. Some original parts such as rings, bearings, camshafts, gasket sets, carburetor rebuild kits, water pumps, oil pumps, and the like may still be available from your local auto parts store. Depending on the year of your collector car, a surprising number of parts may also be available from the manufacturer.

You say you need hubcaps for your Mustang? No problem! You'd be surprised how many hubcaps have stories behind them.

Unfortunately, ordering the parts you need through a local dealership may pose some challenges. It will probably be helpful to the staff at the parts department if you find a way (volunteer) to look up the part numbers yourself, make a list, and then leave it for the parts people to check availability and get back to you. Finding a friendly counterman may take some time, but it can be worth the effort. And remember, it doesn't hurt to tip them for their time and effort. That will make it a lot easier when you go back in for future orders.

Shiny, gleaming emblems help to make your car complete. Your best bet is to get originals and recondition them, if needed.

REPRODUCTION PARTS

During the last 25 years or so, there has been a tremendous growth in the number of companies that reproduce original parts for collector cars. Many companies specialize in particular makes, such as the Mustang, and offer a complete line of restoration parts ranging from sheet metal to trim, from interior soft parts to engine accessory brackets and emblems. These vendors can be found in *Hemmings* and many enthusiast magazines, as well as in national club newsletters.

SHOWS AND SWAP MEETS

Part of the fun of restoring an old car is the hunt for rare and elusive parts. Throughout the year, major swap meets in Carlisle, PA (www.carsatcarlisle.com), and Pomona, CA (www.pomonaswap-meet.com), draw thousands of vendors and tens of thousands of buyers. There are also hundreds of small, local swap meets that take place, and are likely to draw enthusiasts with parts to spare or trade. There's no telling where or when that elusive part will turn up, so pay attention to notices put out by national and local clubs or flyers for meets of local clubs or enthusiasts. Just be thoroughly familiar with what it is you need and carefully check out any part you are considering buying, to make sure it is correct and in good condition.

CLUBS

When it comes to parts and information, the best investment you can make is to join a local or national club that specializes in Mustangs, such as the Mustang Club of America or the Shelby

American Automobile Club for Shelby Mustang owners. Members of these clubs are usually generous with technical support, and there's always the chance that the parts you need may be listed for sale in the club newsletter.

You can also advertise for the parts you need in the club newsletter. National clubs put on annual show and swap meets. These present the opportunity to not only hunt for parts but also look over restored versions of your car and pick the owners' brains. Car collectors are always eager to talk about their restorations and share their knowledge. They can answer many of your questions about suppliers for parts or the best professionals for specialized work.

JUNKYARDS

Back in the early days of the collector car hobby, junkyards were a great place to find parts and accessories. Now with suburbia spilling out into rural areas where junkyards once thrived, imposition of environmental regulations, and the popularity of crushing old cars for recycling, finding a junkyard with a mother lode of parts is rare. Out in the hinterlands old-time junkyards still exist, and if you can find one intact, there might be good pickings. You may even find a good parts car to cannibalize to complete your restoration.

GROUNDUP RESTORATION

By definition, a "ground-up" or "body-off" restoration entails disassembling the entire car, repairing and rebuilding each component to a like-new condition, and then reassembling it. The restoration process requires that as many original components as possible be utilized, not just for originality, but because these parts are date coded. In a concours restoration, judges will inspect as many components as possible. Alternators, wiper motor covers, steering boxes, exhaust manifolds, and rear axles are just some of the parts that are date coded. If you're doing a concours restoration, it's essential these original parts be rebuilt, restored, and re-installed in the car.

METHODS AND PROCEDURES

How you begin your restoration is up to you. If your budget allows you to do both the mechanical and cosmetic work simultaneously, the restoration will go much faster. If this is not an option, consider completing the mechanicals first, then body and paint, and finally interior.

"Haw, haw, haw! That sure is a beat up Mustang!" Well, I showed them six months later. Sure, the Mustang had four different colors for fenders, but it didn't have any rust. It restored into a beautiful 1968 Shelby Mustang Cobra GT350.

The Shelby from the front. I did change the wheels for the photograph.

Some collectors just drop a car off at a restoration shop, and pick up a completed, restored gem a few months later. This is not the norm. Others don't mind getting dirty from time to time and have an affinity for engines and hard mechanical repair. Still other owner/restorers are intimidated by engines and stick to trim items and bodywork. When you sit down to plan your restoration be realistic about what you are comfortable doing and what drives you absolutely crazy. It's better to farm out or swap a restoration job you don't like to someone who feels comfortable doing it, rather than risk spending more time and money than necessary because you are frustrated.

Whatever course you decide on there are certain things to keep track of. Organization is the key to restoration. Many owner/restorers start a journal of notes and photographs to keep track of the progress in each area of the restoration. Ideally, all the different segments (powertrain, chassis, and body) will be completed at the same time, so the assembly of the car can be handled without interruption.

ENGINE

Most restorations have the engine high up on the list for rebuilding. However, if the miles are low or it has been rebuilt previously, minor surgery may be all that's needed. Unfortunately, there is no guarantee the rebuild was done correctly with top-quality parts, so check engine condition and performance carefully. The last thing you want is to drive your freshly restored car to a show, only to have the engine give up the ghost in the middle of the show field.

Does It Need Rebuilding?

Before removing the engine from the car and disassembling it, find out what the engine's overall condition is. Are there any unusual noises? Does it smoke? Does it make power? If you aren't mechanically inclined, have a reputable mechanic analyze it and give you a report that includes a compression check. Low compression is an indication of worn valves and bad piston rings.

Engine noises are obvious signs of trouble. Valvetrain clacking, for example, can indicate rocker arms need adjustment or defective hydraulic lifters. A heavy thudding or knocking sound can indicate bad main bearings. An engine with valvetrain noises can run for a while but bottom-end noises indicate impending doom. Automotive manuals such as those from Motor and Chilton's usually have a section on noise diagnostics, while most of the repair manuals commonly found in stores don't.

Oil burning and low compression are good reasons for rebuilding an engine. With the exception of

It's amazing what you find inside an engine. This 302 actually still ran with all that junk inside it. It's much better to have it professionally rebuilt.

The same basic 302 after the reconditioning process. Now the fun starts with the paint!

some major machining operations, this is within the realm of the backyard mechanic, provided you have the necessary tools and literature.

If you do decide on an engine rebuild, it might be wise to have hardened exhaust valve seats installed in the cylinder heads. That decision really depends on how you plan to drive your car but if it will see drag strip action or be used to tow an RV across the country, then hardened valve seats are highly recommended. Also, thankfully, for average driving, pre-1972 Mustangs do just fine running on today's unleaded gas.

Farming Out

It is also well within the capabilities of the average owner to remove the engine from the car, take it apart, and then drop it off at the machine shop. Subsidiary components, such as the carburetor, distributor, starter, and alternator, can be rebuilt and detailed at home. Of course, you can drop these off too and have them rebuilt professionally. Always have the original parts rebuilt, if possible, rather than get replacement parts which might not have the correct original part numbers and date codes.

Certain parts, such as most modern fuel pumps, might not be readily rebuildable, so you might have to locate an original part in good condition, which might not be an easy task.

ENGINE DETAILS

Once you have the engine out, you can decide what to do with the air conditioning system, power steering, power brake booster, radiator, and any other underhood accessory (assuming your car has them). If they work fine, perhaps just a thorough cleaning and repaint is all that's required, particularly parts that are still in good, serviceable condition. On some components, it doesn't pay to cut corners; it would be wise to have the radiator boiled out, for example, no matter what its condition is.

If you are not doing a complete, body-off restoration, it is considerably easier to restore the engine compartment once the engine is out. It is also much easier to work on the front suspension with the engine out of the way. Once you get the engine out, spend some time detailing it, especially the areas that will be hard to reach once it is back in the engine compartment. Many auto parts stores carry engine paint.

It's also just plain common sense to replace the original hoses, fan belts, and spark plug wires with new ones. Today, correct replacement parts are available for collector cars that duplicate the original codes, markings, and colors. If reproductions are not offered, duplicating the makings, codes, and colors from the originals can be done. There is usually someone who knows how in Mustang clubs.

WIRING AND ELECTRICAL SYSTEMS

If you need sheet metal, you may find it at a large swap meet, such as this one held at Carlisle, PA..

Electrical systems can be hard to work with because wiring diagrams are not easy to read and decipher. On cars that are loaded with electrically operated options, all you have to do is to look underneath the dash to get discouraged. There are big bundles of differently colored wires that are hard to follow and trace.

If your car has electrical problems, you must first familiarize yourself with the circuit, isolate the problem, and then repair the wiring or replace the defective electrical component. This is easier said than done. If you're uncertain about working with electrical circuits, study a book dealing with automotive electrical systems, such as HPBooks' Automotive Electrical Handbook, before you attempt any repairs. Also study the car's wiring diagrams, which may be available from the dealer. Remember that all wires are color coded, and wiring harnesses are like the trunk and branches of a tree. As the harness branches out to the various accessories and circuits, by following the color codes it's easier to trace and repair problems than you might think.

The most common problems when repairing electrical wiring are dry-rotted insulation and driveway jerry-rigging. These pose a safety hazard and your wiring harness should be repaired. If it's beyond repair, you'll have to replace it. Fortunately, there are a number of companies that sell reproduction wiring harnesses for most American cars. Refer to Appendix 3 for resources.

STEERING AND DRIVETRAIN

The drivetrain consists of the transmission, driveshaft, and rear axle. It is probably more cost- and time-effective to send these components out for repair and/or reconditioning than to invest in the many specialized tools required to rebuild them.

TRANSMISSIONS

If your car is equipped with a manual transmission, remember to have the flywheel balanced and turned. Also consider upgrading to one of the newer clutch styles now offered by Hayes. If it is equipped with automatic transmission, be careful that the rebuild shop doesn't replace your unit with a rebuilt transmission. The original transmission is date coded. You'll lose originality if you settle for a replacement.

REAR AXLE

Make sure the rear axle ring and pinion are inspected for wear, and if it's a limited slip, that the C-clips are in good shape. Have new axle bearings pressed on and request that the rear be set up by an experienced mechanic.

STEERING BOX

Unless you're an above average mechanic, the same advice applies for both manual and power steering boxes. However, you should be able to do a good job of detailing them prior to installation. There are a number of reference books that provide detailing information from Classic Motorbooks (www.mbi.com).

One of the most fun things about this hobby is looking for parts. You never know what you'll find.

It might look as though these boxes are filled with automotive junk, but for someone in the know, the boxes might contain what they need for their restoration.

FRONT AND REAR SUSPENSION

Suspension work is essentially an R & R (remove and replace) operation, and is well within the reach of the average enthusiast. Some specialized tools are usually required, particularly when it comes to removing ball joints and springs, but these aren't very expensive.

It is absolutely essential that care be taken when working with coil springs. These components are under tremendous tension and removing them incorrectly can lead to severe personal injury. Therefore, when removing coil springs, always use a coilspring compressor.

SUSPENSION UPGRADES

There are many companies that offer complete suspension rebuild kits consisting of all the necessary parts needed to revitalize your car's suspension. This is one area where you may want to upgrade from stock parts if you're not too concerned about originality. Polyurethane bushings for control arms and anti-roll bars outlast rubber parts and also improve handling. The improved handling and steering control will give you a much safer and more pleasurable ride.

BRAKES

Don't skimp on the braking system. If equipped with drum brakes, make sure the drums are turned and trued. Don't try to reuse old parts—get rid of the old springs and wheel cylinders, and replace with all new units. However, if a concours restoration is your goal, you should rebuild the old cylinders, because they are date coded.

Many novice enthusiasts are confused about the difference between standard brake fluid and silicone fluid. Silicone fluid is an excellent choice if the car is to see limited service, as it tends to resist water better. It is more expensive and it's important to realize that standard brake fluid cannot be added to a system filled with silicone fluid.

An area of the braking system that sometimes gets overlooked is the brake lines. Inspect every inch of the lines for leaking, and replace all rubber lines leading to the wheel cylinders. Inspect the master cylinder and have it rebuilt if necessary. Finally, make sure the parking brake is in good working order and that the cables are not frayed or damaged.

TIRES

Tires, of course, are part of your car's suspension system. If you are into strict originality, most classic and original model tires are available as reproductions but many enthusiasts use modern radials instead. A compromise is to use radials for driving because they are safer and improve ride quality and handling, and keep a set of stock original tires to put on for car shows.

INTERIOR, UPHOLSTERY, AND TRIM

Here is another area where even the novice can get in and do a good job. Many companies offer the products and kits necessary to make minor repairs. There are also many reproduction interior kits available from various companies.

Carpets

There is nothing like a new set of carpets to rejuvenate an interior. At least, it is a good starting place and they are fairly easy to replace. Reproduction carpeting is readily available and while you are at it, replace the padding too. If the carpet is fine but just needs a thorough cleaning, there are a variety of cleaners available that will do the job.

Door Panels and Dash Pads

Door panel replacement is also quite easy. There are a number of companies that offer reproduction door and quarter trim panels. You'll need to transfer any bright moldings and emblems from the old panel to the new, but this is a simple process. Dash pad replacement can be a little more difficult, especially in late sixties and early seventies models. Care must be taken not to damage the pads. Make sure you use plenty of protectant like Armor All, or Meguiar's Intensive Protectant to soften the pads to avoid cracking.

Seats

When it comes to reupholstering your car's seats, you're better off leaving this job to a professional reupholsterer. To save some money, try to locate and obtain the material yourself to avoid surcharge fees the reupholsterer may add. Virtually all cars have reproduction upholstery available, and it isn't very expensive. Lack of experience recovering seats may lead to a costly mistake, though. If reproduction upholstery isn't available, redying original upholstery that is in good shape may be an

Typical for a 1966 Mustang in need of restoration. It needs a lot of work, but they all do, don't they?

option. The advantage of redying is that you can assemble pieces from several cars (even if they are different colors) and redye them to look factory fresh. The same goes for headliners.

Vinyl

Vinyl rips and tears can sometimes be repaired very effectively. Local reupholstery shops can usually do the job, or contact your local car dealer. There are vinyl repairmen who visit dealerships from time to time, repairing rips and tears on trade-ins. Their skill in matching the liquid vinyl color and grain is light years ahead of what an amateur can do. There are several kits available that will help you repair minor tears yourself.

Instrument Panel

While the interior is apart, disassemble the instrument panel and clean and inspect the instruments. There are a number of companies that provide a rebuilding service for those that are not working.

Radios can also be serviced. Replacement speakers are available from just about any electronics store that stocks car audio components, and should be installed behind original speaker covers where possible.

CHROME-PLATED TRIM PARTS

Chrome-plated trim parts, whether exterior or interior, may have to be removed and sent out for replating. You may be able to find usable replacements at swap meets or, as is the case with certain popular cars, reproduced replacement parts might be available. Remember that you probably won't be able to match up rechromed and NOS (new-old-stock) pieces. NOS chrome is no match for show chrome, so plan on sending everything out for replating.

Painted trim and moldings that are worn will need to be repainted. You'll probably end up painting all the moldings to insure a correct match because with most cars, the original paint has faded.

197

BODYWORK AND PAINT

Peel the carpet off, and you're greeted by the additional "ventilation hole" by your feet. When you find a gaping hole like this, do some serious thinking. A hole like this can only be repaired in one of two ways. The first is to cut the rusted area out and weld in sheet metal to cover it. The other is to replace the entire floorpan of the car. Both options are expensive.

More than anything else, it is your car's bodywork and paint that will be noticed and judged by others. This can mean different things to different people. For someone who is restoring a car with originality as the goal, any imperfections that the car came with from the factory will be left untouched or will be reproduced when repainted.

Few cars left the assembly plant without some paint runs or overspray. A dedicated restoration will attempt to duplicate these errors. Others prefer to improve upon what the factory produced and will end up with bodywork and paint that is considerably better than new. A great paint job looks almost alive, with a liquid quality that seems to flow over every part of the body. It is unique and incredibly satisfying. However, a great paint job cannot hide body imperfections, and will in fact draw attention to them.

Paint Removal

Before the painting can be done, the old paint must be removed down to the bare metal. The recommended process is to use a chemical stripper to remove the old paint and primer. Care must be used with chemical strippers. Only work in a well-ventilated area and never use the stripper in direct sunlight. Be prepared to do lots of scraping and scouring to get all the old paint off. Make sure you wear goggles, a mask over your nose and mouth, and rubber gloves, as well as clothing to protect your skin. Paint stripper is volatile and toxic stuff.

An alternative to stripping is to have the body, frame, and other painted parts dipped in a chemical bath. In this process, the entire body is immersed in a large vat filled with chemical removing agents.

Dipping has a lot to recommend it but there are drawbacks. On one hand, it simplifies the paint removal process and certainly will remove all paint and primer, as well as any chemical impurities in the metal. On the other hand, failure to remove the chemical agent completely during the rinse process can result in it continuing to eat away at the metal, even after the car is painted. There's no guarantee that the chemical agents will entirely be flushed out of the myriad nooks and crevices of a car's body. Refer to Appendix 3 for resources for chemical stripping products and companies. Redi Strip (main office: 9910 Jordon Circle, Santa Fe Springs, CA 90670; 213-944-9915) has 23 facilities across the country that offer chemical dipping.

Body Inspection

Once the body is down to bare metal, the inspection process begins, and here great attention to detail is an absolute must. Rust is insidious; it can eat away at metal in both exposed and hidden areas. Carefully inspect every inch of the exterior and interior. Climb into the trunk and check the cavities down in the lower quarters. The cowl and the area under the front windshield are examples of areas very prone to rust.

Depending on the rust or collision damage, you may or may not have to replace sheet metal. Fortunately, reproduction sheet metal is offered for most Mustang models, but here the buyer must be careful about the source. Over the past few years, offshore sheet metal, mostly from Asia, has become more popular in the collision repair business, and many reproduction panels are now made of this same type of metal. The problem is that the alloy steel used contains impurities not found in pure steel sheet metal. The acid and other impurities in the imported steel actually eat at the metal and bubble under the paint, eventually ruining both.

Used Sheet Metal

One alternative to replacing trunk pans, floor pans, quarter panels, and fenders with reproduction or NOS parts is to use used sheet metal. There are a number of companies that offer sheet metal

This Mustang looks worse than it really is. If the body is solid, it's a matter of removing the old interior and replacing it with a new one.

199

"Mustang Restoration" features reprinted articles from "Hot Rod Magazine." It's worth taking a look. www.hotrod.com

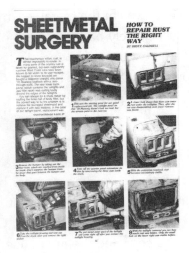

This is a sample article from "Mustang Restoration," by Bruce Caldwell.

from the Southwest that is rust free and quite affordable. These companies advertise in publications such as *Hemmings* (www.hemmings.com).

It's much easier to work on body panels when they are removed from the car. It's difficult work, requiring respirators, goggles, and a well-ventilated area.

Preparation

Whether you do it yourself or have the car painted professionally, the key to a good paint job is in the preparation. Under close inspection the effects of any shortcuts taken are noticeable after the high of seeing your car repainted wears off. The preparation of the metal surface is just the first step in a quality paint job.

Another concern is the use of plastic body filler or Bondo. Plastic filler is not a good substitute for lead or metal. It is best used to smooth the metal surface prior to sanding and priming. Sanding the surface well before the first coats of primer are laid down is also important. Many painters also prefer to use different colors of primer between coats. Applying different colored coats of primer helps show high spots that need correction because the primer beneath will show through.

Types of Paint

Today's restorer also has choices as to what paint to use. If a concours restoration is the goal, then he is obligated to use the same type of paint as on the original car. For example, most American cars of the fifties, sixties, and seventies used lacquer, so in restoring a car of that era correctly, the paint of choice would have to be lacquer. There are, however, a variety of other paints now available that look as good as lacquer, are as easy to apply, and are far more durable.

If the body panel can't be repaired or replaced, then a replacement has to be made. This task requires basic metal fabrication skills. Sure, you can do it yourself, but replacement body panels for Mustangs are readily available.

A looming problem is that use of lacquer is slowly being phased out due to pollution considerations. Today, polyurethanes and base coat/clear coat paints are more popular and provide excellent gloss and durability. Take the time to explore your choices and ask for recommendations from professionals who have done this type of restoration work before. Your decision should be based on how you want your car to ultimately be identified: as a stock model, concours level restoration, or as an individual representation of the make and model year. If the choice is to go concours, then repaint with the correct type of paint. If you're not a slave to restoration, the sky's the limit.

As far as ensuring correctness for color, restorers can now use spectroscopic analysis to achieve authenticity. One restorer recommends matching to a spot under the trunk lid since this area is unlikely to be affected by normal fading or corruption from exposure to acid rain or other environmental forces.

Applying Paint

When it comes to painting the car yourself, unless you have experience, pass this job on to a professional. When you get right down to it, painting is an art, with many variables. Having the right equipment is essential. Besides the large amounts of dust and residue that accumulate with the many sanding and resanding steps, paints and solvents are extremely toxic and require a well-ventilated yet sealed work area.

16
Basic Mustang Maintenance

A restored classic car will require just as much maintenance as a modern vehicle that is driven daily. The way it is maintained while it's sitting pretty will be just as important as when it is on the road. Protecting the finish with wax is a good first step but simple, preventative maintenance on the drivetrain should also be rigorously followed. It's really the best way of protecting your investment.

OIL CHANGES

Prompt, regular oil changes are important for your collector car. Many collectors avoid driving their cars by trailering them to shows. This is a good idea because it saves wear on the tires, keeps the cars super clean, and odometer mileage stays low. Changing the oil every 2,000–3,000 miles or, at the very least, twice a year, is still recommended. This is necessary because when oil is exposed to air it begins to oxidize.

Synthetic Oil

It is also worth considering switching over to a synthetic oil such as Mobil 1, Quaker State, or Pennzoil. Synthetic oils offer several advantages. For example, unlike conventional motor oils, synthetics can withstand considerably higher temperatures, to the order of 700 degrees as opposed to

After all the hard work and expense that went into your restoration, it only makes sense to maintain your Mustang by servicing it regularly and storing it properly.

You may want to consider using a synthetic engine oil, like Mobil, Synthetic ATF, Mobil, Extended Performance, or Pennzoil, Platinum, for several reasons. Synthetics can withstand nearly twice the oil temperature as regular oil and also have superior lubricating properties.

300–350 degrees for petroleum-based lubricants. This is important, because the upper cylinder areas of an engine reach temperatures in the 600-degree range. Conventional oils will begin to break down and oxidize almost immediately. Oxidation occurs when the hot oil is exposed to the air, which then leads to the formation of organic acids that combine and form varnish deposits, tar, and sludge. That is why frequent changes are recommended with conventional oils, while synthetics, because they don't break down as quickly, can go much longer between changes.

In addition, synthetics have much higher film strength, which results in much less blow-by past the piston rings, again reducing oil contamination. Synthetics also lower temperatures in the crankcase and because they are slipperier, mileage improves. An additional benefit for the collector car that isn't driven often is that synthetics also have the distinct advantage of having an affinity for metal. They adhere to internal metal engine parts, unlike conventional oils that drain off very quickly. If the car sits for extended periods of time, a synthetic provides considerably more protection and prevents damage from so-called "dry" starts.

Drain Plugs

Another wise modification is to replace the original drain plug with a magnetic one in the oil pan. This is an inexpensive way to prevent small metal particles from circulating in the oil, by having them cling to the magnetic plug instead. When the plug is removed to drain the oil, simply clean the metal particles from the plug, and reinstall once the pan is drained.

COOLANT

The coolant in your radiator should be changed every two years or so, with a 50-50 ratio of water to antifreeze; putting in any more antifreeze is not recommended. Although antifreeze raises the boiling point of water by 15 degrees (with a 15-lb. pressure cap), and protects against freezing, antifreeze inhibits heat absorption and slows the rate by which the water/antifreeze mixture releases heat.

When changing the antifreeze, make sure that the rest of the cooling system is in good condition. Check all the hoses, clamps, and the radiator cap. Soft hoses should be replaced. When flushing the cooling system, use a reverse flow flushing kit (such as the one offered by Prestone). Reversing the flow of water through the various passages of the cooling system will remove scale and rust that may not be removed by flushing in only one direction. Once the system is flushed, remove the heater hose with the reverse-flow valve and install a new heater hose. Keep the old hose for the next time you flush the system.

Coolant should be replaced every two years regardless of how often you drive your car. Here are two examples, Zerex, and Prestone,. Extended Life coolant (Prestone, on the right) does last longer. Also frequently check all other areas of the cooling system, such as belts, hoses, clamps, and the radiator cap.

OTHER FLUID LEVELS

The fluids used in the power steering pump, automatic transmission, manual transmission, and rear axle should all be changed when you first get your car or as part of the restoration. Again, synthetic fluids are available for all these applications and are recommended. Check these fluid levels each time the car is to be driven, at each oil change, or at least every six months.

MANUAL TRANSMISSION

Manual transmission and rear axle fluids don't have to changed often. Every 75,000-100,000 miles is an acceptable interval because these heavy oils deteriorate very slowly. The only time you want to change them more often is if the car is used for heavy service, such as racing or trailer-towing. Check their levels every six months.

AUTOMATIC TRANSMISSION

Cars equipped with an automatic transmission should have the fluid changed every 15,000 miles and the filter every 30,000 miles. If during the course of driving, the car overheats, check the transmission fluid immediately. Most automatic transmission oil coolers are routed through the lower radiator tank; an overheated engine could cause the automatic transmission fluid to also overheat and lead to transmission failure.

TUNE-UPS

Unless the engine is rebuilt when the car is restored, perform a major tune-up before you begin driving the car. It's much easier to follow a maintenance schedule thereafter because you are starting with a freshly tuned engine.

Major Tune-ups

This Shelby 428 c.i. engine has dual carburetors, known for their finickey tuning. Frequent engine maintenance is required for engines like these for maximum performance.

A major tune-up includes new spark plugs, points, condenser (if so equipped), distributor cap, rotor, and spark plug wires. Change the oil, oil filter, air filter, fuel filter, PCV valve and hose, and all vacuum hoses. Set the timing, adjust the carburetor's idle speed, adjust the fuel mixture, and choke and lubricate all the throttle and carburetor linkages. If the car is equipped with emissions equipment (EGR, air pump, and so on), make sure these are in good working order. Adjust the valve lash on engines equipped with solid lifter camshafts, according to settings found generally in a Chilton's or Haynes engine manual. Finally, adjust the clutch or check the vacuum lines to the automatic transmission.

Minor Tune-up

Every six months in perpetuity, a minor tune-up will be necessary. A minor tune-up involves checking the timing and the carburetor, inspecting the filters, and topping off all the fluid levels.

Frequency

A major tune-up should be performed every two years or 24,000 miles thereafter; a minor tune-up every six months. It may not be necessary to change all the components specified above, especially if you only drive the car 2,000–3,000 miles per year, but they should be inspected at regular intervals to keep the engine running at peak performance.

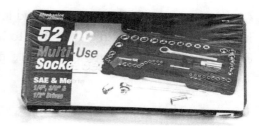

It's also a good idea to carry a tool set in your trunk. You never know when it'll come in handy. This set is from Mechanics Products,.

Certain high-horsepower muscle car-era engines, such as the 428 Shelby, came with two carburetors and some, like the 289, had a solid lifter camshaft. The 428 is known for its ability to frequently go out of tune. These engines require constant tuning for optimum performance.

It's a good idea to have a professional, reputable mechanic check out your car with diagnostic equipment as part of the major tuneup.

Other Underhood Maintenance

All accessory drive belts should be checked at every oil change for correct belt tension. This information can be found in the factory service manual or a Chilton's repair manual (for you vehicle). Inspect the underside of the belts for any fraying and cracking, and replace any that look suspect.

BATTERY

Unless it's a maintenance-free battery, check each cell for proper electrolytic levels and fill with distilled water only. Make sure the battery cables are routed away from the exhaust manifolds and use a battery brush tool to clean the terminals and clamps at least once a year.

MISCELLANEOUS BOLTS

Tighten down the valve cover bolts, timing cover bolts, and oil pan bolts once a year. These have a habit of loosening, resulting in oil leaks. If so equipped, have the air conditioning system checked out professionally and recharged once a year.

BRAKE FLUID

Check the brake master cylinder fluid level at every oil change and every time your car is tuned up. It is normal for cars with disc brakes to have the fluid level fall slightly as the pads wear, but cars with drum brakes on all four wheels should not show any drop in fluid level.

CHASSIS AND BODY

All suspension points should be lubricated and checked for damage and wear every six months or 12,000 miles. A grease gun is all you'll need to do this yourself. Make sure that any car equipped with ball joints has grease fittings. If not, you can purchase these at any parts store, thread them in, and then use a synthetic grease to lubricate them. A car equipped with manual steering should have its box's fluid level checked every six months.

It is also important to have your wheel bearings checked and repacked with fresh grease at least once a year or every 12,000 miles.

BRAKES

Once again, start fresh by having new pads or shoes installed before the car hits the road. Consider switching to silicone brake fluid, as it is less prone to brake line corrosion and won't become contaminated if moisture enters the brake system. Have the rotors and drums cut, and use semi-metallic pads

Brakes should be checked every 30,000 miles or so, but visually check the pads and shoes every six months. Rotors and drums should be turned (machined) when you replace the pads and shoes. Suspension and steering pickup points should be lubricated every time you change the oil.

or linings as they will last longer. Install new brake cylinders (or if the wheel cylinders are date coded in your concours car, rebuild them), have the calipers rebuilt, and use all new brake hardware.

Make sure that the parking brake works and that all brake lines are in good condition. It is hard to say how long your brakes will last from then on, but under normal driving, you can expect to get 30,000 miles. Visually inspect the pads and shoes at least every six months.

BODY LUBRICATION

Use a high-quality, multipurpose grease or smooth white body type lubricant at least once a year on the hood hinges and latch, fuel filler door, door and trunk hinges, and door latches. Use graphite for the lock cylinders, at least once a year. Lubricate the parking brake assembly and other items such as ashtray slides and concealed headlight doors, if so equipped.

STORAGE

Since most collector cars are spared the abuse of winter driving, the question of proper storage always comes up. As a general rule, it is much better to drive your car occasionally rather than to put it away in long-term storage, since all of the fluids circulate and the moisture that accumulates in the engine can then be burned off. Oils, fluids, and gasoline all deteriorate in time, breaking down and creating sludge and varnish. However, in areas where winters are harsh, cars are often put away until spring.

What constitutes short-term versus long-term storage? Six months or less is considered short term, while anything longer is long term and requires additional steps.

THE GARAGE

The ideal place to store a vehicle is in a well-lit, heated garage that has a wooden floor. A wooden floor absorbs moisture, thereby reducing the possibility of rust formation. Heat does the same thing, but its benefits are more readily apparent in the colder, damper months. Heat dissipates moisture and dries the air out. Most garages have cement floors which absorb moisture but also release it rather quickly. To ameliorate this, plastic sheathing can be placed on the floor and then covered with plywood. The plastic acts as a moisture barrier, and the wood absorbs any moisture that gets past the plastic. Bags of silica gel placed in the garage also help absorb moisture.

BATTERY

Some owners prefer to remove the battery from the car, while others just remove the positive cable. Leaving the battery in the car could result in corrosion from the battery eating away at the supporting box or tray. Also, an electrical component may fail or a wire could short (even without the key in the ignition), causing a major short-circuit and subsequent fire. If the battery is removed, do not place it directly on a cement floor as the battery will quickly discharge. Instead, place it on a thick piece of wood.

BLOCKS

One of the big questions regarding storage is whether or not to put the car on blocks and if so, where to place the blocks—under the frame or the suspension. The best way is to jack the car up using a quality floor jack and then place quality jack stands under the front and rear suspension points. Remove the tires and stack them in a corner, placing cardboard between each one, and then cover them to prevent fading.

OTHER DETAILS

Place a tray or several sheets of corrugated cardboard under the oil pan to catch any oil that might leak; you can also put newspapers underneath the engine compartment and transmission to help absorb and pinpoint any possible leaks.

Any time a car is placed in storage, even short term, clean all the windows inside and out, and empty and clean all the ashtrays. Don't put any additional protectant on weather stripping anywhere in or outside the car as the moisture in the protectant will attract mold and mildew. Place a handful of mothballs in a tin pie plate and set one on both the front and rear floors of the interior and put another in the trunk. You may also want to seal the tailpipes to stop rats and mice from taking up winter residence.

Always have a fully charged fire extinguisher handy; this is usually an insurance requirement anyway. And if your car is particularly valuable, a security system may also be a good idea. It really doesn't pay to skimp when it comes to fire prevention and security.

LONG-TERM STORAGE

In addition to the precautions taken for short-term storage, long-term storage requires additional procedures be performed. The gas tank must be drained and the car should be run until all the gasoline remaining in the fuel lines and carburetor is used.

Remove each spark plug and squirt oil in each cylinder, then reinstall the spark plugs. A lightweight oil or graphite grease should also be used on all body lubrication points. A car cover should be used, and the battery removed and stored elsewhere.

REMOVAL FROM STORAGE

When the time comes to take the car out of long-term storage, make sure the battery is fully charged. It can be taken to a service station, checked out, and charged or, if you have a trickle charger, put it on the night before it's to be installed.

Check all fluid levels and tire pressure. You may also want to squirt some oil in each cylinder to prevent a dry start. Before you start the car up, change the oil and pour a few gallons of gasoline into the tank. Also pour about half a cup of gasoline down the carburetor bores. Disconnect the coil wire to prevent the engine from starting and crank the engine to pump oil up into the lifters and valve train.

Now connect the coil wire and start the engine. When it starts, don't rev the engine until it is fully warmed up. Check the fuel pressure gauge or lamp, then look for any leaks in the engine compartment. Also check to see that everything works, including wipers, lights, and any power accessories.

Be sure to coat the tires with a rubber protectant prior to long-term storage. Check the pressures periodically and keep them correct. This is especially important before you drive the car after it has been stored for a long time.

211

Drive the car slowly and pump the brakes; they may jab initially. Finally, after the drive, check again for any fluid leaks in the engine compartment and look under the car for any transmission and axle leaks. If there are leaks, this can indicate dried-out gaskets or loose hold-down bolts. Tighten any clamps and hold-down bolts to see if that stops the leaks. If not, you'll probably have to replace the gaskets.

CAR COVERS

There are many types of covers available to choose from. Even though collector cars aren't driven much, they still need protection from dust and other outside debris, especially when they are in storage. Car covers are available specifically for all types of models or you can save a few dollars by getting a size that fits cars approximately the same size as yours.

The most important consideration when purchasing a cover is selecting the right kind of fabric for your specific storage application.

Types of Fabrics

Cotton flannel fabrics breathe, allowing air to circulate through them. They are soft and easy on the car's paint and wax. They have no fluid resistance so they should only be used in the dry environment of a garage.

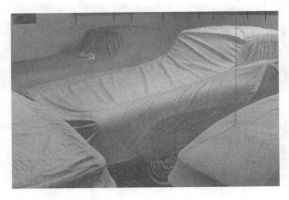

The most important consideration when choosing a car cover is the fabric. Composite covers made of several layers of breathing and absorbing materials are the best.

Cotton polyester fabrics have poor fluid resistance and they trap heat and moisture. Their stiffness can harm your paint and remove wax and they can also fade. When they are treated with a chemical repellent, they lose their ability to breathe.

Nylon fabrics have the same deficiencies as cotton polyester fabrics.

Plastic films should be avoided because they don't breathe, and they trap heat and moisture. Here again, stiffness can damage the paint. They shrink in the cold and stretch in the heat, and provide only minimal hail and nick protection. Vinyl films should be avoided for the same reasons.

Composite covers made from several layers of material combine the best of each type. For example, covers made from Kimberly-Clark's Evolution 3 fabric are made in four layers. These allow the cover to breathe, repel fluids, and provide protection against hail and nicks. Another benefit is that an Evolution 3 cover will not rot or become mildewed if folded and stored while it is wet.

If you only plan to use a cover in the garage, then a simple cotton cover is sufficient. For a car kept outside or that will be trailered, the Evolution 3 fabric will provide the best of all worlds to keep the car's finish clean, dry, and scratch-free.

17
Basic Mustang Detailing

Most of the driving public takes the time to wax their car only once or twice a year. A collector car requires and deserves much more than an occasional wash and waxing. As the name implies, detailing means cleaning, polishing, and waxing all the details. It's painstaking work. Like everything else that is related to collector cars, detailing requires a big initial investment in terms of time and effort, followed by regular maintenance. Detailing is a task in which each piece of metal, glass, rubber, and vinyl is cleaned and polished until it gleams. The engine compartment and undercarriage are made absolutely sanitary, and the interior sparkles from carpet to headliner. Dirt simply does not exist after a thorough detailing. For many, getting the car to look better than the day it left the dealer is the goal. If you only drive the car occasionally, maintaining that look isn't a problem once you get to that point.

Even the most mechanically inept enthusiast can detail his or her car. How much time and effort is required depends on the level of perfection you want, and the amount of time you want to spend driving your collector Mustang.

Detailing also means paying attention to the details of your restoration. This means making sure the correct decals and emblems are in place; that all nuts and bolts are fastened securely; and that the

You'll need a complete supply of high quality car care products, such as the ones shown here. (Murphy Oil Soap, Armor All Protectant, Kit Fabric Cleaner, Meguiar's Car Cleaner, The Wax Shop Greaseless Leather, Rubber, Vinyl, No 7 White Polishing Compound, Nevr-Dull Magic Wadding Polish, Crystal White Octagon).

spark plug wires curve properly. In addition to cleaning, detailing includes taking care of all minor imperfections.

CONCOURS DETAILING

For those wishing to enter concours competitions, be forewarned. Just having a car that is as clean as the day it left the dealership won't cut it in a concours competition. Concours cars must be perfect, because the judges look for anything that might be wrong. For example dirt found in the tail light lens housing after the lens is removed is enough for a car to lose points. Spark plug wires that don't curve properly leaving the distributor cap, or radiator fins that aren't perfectly straight, are reasons for losing points. The time and work required to prepare a car for concours competition is enormous. Due to the exacting nature of the concours competition, 99% of all serious concours cars are no longer driven but must be trailered from show to show. Some enthusiasts regard concours competition as being the epitome of nitpicking, while to others it is the ultimate form of automotive appreciation.

A typical major detailing should be done either immediately after the car is acquired or after all mechanical or cosmetic work is completed. Thereafter, it is just a matter of maintenance. Unless you allow the car to get dirty, there is no reason for another major detail to be necessary for at least four months. Keeping areas that attract dirt more than others, such as the wheels, wheel wells, grille, engine compartment, and undercarriage, covered, protected, or somehow away from dust, dirt, and the elements, should be enough. The more you drive the car, the more cleaning and maintenance it will be require. And remember, concours cars are not driven because this is the best way to prevent deterioration and/or damage. If you choose to drive your classic Mustang, it will deteriorate, regardless of how well you maintain it.

DETAILING SHOPS

No collector in his right mind would take a collectible to a detailing shop. Detailing shops are geared toward cleaning and refurbishing cars that are to be sold or driven daily. A quality restoration shop, however, will do a thorough job on all facets of a collector car, leaving no stone unturned in the quest for cleanliness. Remember it's easy to maintain a restored car that isn't driven. A driven car can be detailed, but never to concours specifications. However, a detailing shop can do a stand-up job on a driver that will turn heads on the street. They charge as much as several hundred dollars and take several days, but the results can be outstanding.

Even a professional detailer can miss things, though. It all depends on what you want them to do. Detail shops usually try to give the best, most noticeable results for the money. For example, while an owner may spend an entire day cleaning and dressing the interior, or on just the wheels, the typical detail shop can't be expected to do that. They are capable of doing a decent job but to get the interior of the wheels absolutely perfect may require many, many hours of labor. Detailing also includes things such as the wheel wells and the underbody. Each customer's demands will be different. One person may be happy with a beautiful interior, exterior, and engine but may not want to go beyond that. You have to specify exactly what you want and be willing to pay the bill for the labor and time invested by the detailer.

EXTERIOR DETAILING

Many a serious collector derives hours of enjoyment by honing the appearance of the car personally. All that's needed is the time, the right materials, and a lot of elbow grease.

Assuming you're starting with a dirty, street-driven car, the first step is to coat the lower body sides, wheel wells, and wheels with kerosene. Kerosene won't hurt the paint, but it will dissolve any road grime, dirt, tar, and the like. If one application doesn't do the trick, try as many as it takes. Be careful because kerosene will loosen up and dissolve any undercoating present. Use plenty of water to rinse the kerosene off. If there are particularly stubborn spots, use a bug and tar remover, which contains stronger dissolving agents, with the kerosene.

WASHING

Many detailing manuals recommend using a dish detergent to wash your car. Dish detergents are fine as long as you understand they will strip away any wax or polish on the finish. If you're starting with a dirty car that has road tar and oxidized paint, dish detergent will work well. Once the car has been cleaned and waxed, use one of the many detergents designed to remove dirt but leave the wax finish, like Meguiar's HiTech Wash or Zip Wax car wash, or a similar product from a car care manufacturer.

Washing Procedures

Hose the car down from top to bottom, to loosen surface dirt which can scratch the paint. Also use a soft cotton terrycloth wash mitt, again to avoid scratching the paint. The wash mitt does not absorb dirt particles that will damage the paint finish. Do not use typical household sponges, since they can trap and hold dirt, and then rub it into the surface being washed. The resulting scratches may be small, but cumulatively, will dull the paint. It's also important to constantly rinse the car and empty the bucket or wash pail several times and refill with fresh detergent and clean water.

Avoid washing or waxing a car in the direct sun; water evaporates and leaves water spots. Wash in the shade or during late evening or early morning when the sun is not as strong. Never try to wax a car when the temperature falls below 50 degrees Fahrenheit. When drying, use a quality chamois cloth, followed by a soft Turkish towel.

Wheel wells and brakes should be flushed out and washed with kerosene. Ideally, you'll have done major repair and painting during the restoration process. Thereafter, a thorough cleaning should keep them looking new. How often depends on how much you drive your car.

PAINT CHIPS

At this stage, you may want to take care of any paint chips with a small touch-up paint kit. If the color you need for your car is not available, an automotive paint store should be able to mix some up for you. Automotive paint stores should have the color code listing for your car. If they don't, you can find the color codes listed on the data plate attached to the firewall or cowl, or check with the car dealer or with a car club. If absolutely nothing is available, drive the car to the paint store or remove a painted part and take it to the store and ask them to match it.

TOUCHUP PROCEDURES

Make sure all wax and polish has been removed from the area to be touched up. Using a fine brush, build successive layers of paint on the chip until the painted area is a little higher than the surrounding paint. Let it dry for about a week. Then sand the paint down with #600 or finer wet sandpaper until the painted area is the same level as the rest of the paint. Follow up with several applications of sealer and glaze and wait at least a month for the paint to cure before you wax the affected area.

WAKING UP SLEEPING PAINT

When the exterior is clean you'll be able to see what condition the paint is in. If your car's paint looks dull and doesn't have much shine, that indicates the top layer of paint has oxidized. There is nothing you can do to bring that layer of paint back; all you can do is remove it, exposing the healthy paint below. By removing the dead paint layer, you'll also remove light scratches, water spots, and swirl marks. The trick here is knowing how much paint to remove and what materials to use. Thereafter, the wax layer inhibits further oxidation while allowing the paint to breathe.

FINISH RESTORERS

If the paint surface is in good condition, all you may need is a finish restorer. Most of these, like Turtle Wax's Color Back, come in liquid form, which makes them easy to apply. Stronger than a wax or polish, but not as strong as rubbing compound, finish restorers remove very light oxidation, grime, tar, and light swirl marks. However, they generally don't offer much in the way of wax protection. Meguiar's Car Cleaner Wax, has three cleaners: fine-cut, medium-cut, and heavy-cut, to safely remove surface defects. The one you choose depends on the severity of the defects. After that, a thorough waxing is in order.

You may get away with using a sealer and glaze on moderately oxidized paint. The fine grit in the polish removes surface imperfections. After using one of these products, follow up with a good carnauba waxing.

RUBBING COMPOUNDS

Unless the paint surface is severely oxidized and has deep scratches, avoid using rubbing compounds. The danger here is that the harshness of the abrasives can abrade the surface down to the primer, necessitating new paint. Use rubbing compounds only as a last resort. If you can't save the paint by compounding, a paint job is unavoidable.

WAXING AND POLISHING

The terms "waxing" and "polishing" today are interchangeable. When using waxes, make sure the product is compatible with the condition of your car's surface. Unless otherwise specified, all waxes contain a mild abrasive to remove surface oxidation. Unless your paint surface is brand new or nearly new, these products are fine. If, however the paint is new or nearly new, use a non-abrasive wax, such as Turtle Wax's NonAbrasive car wax.

Generally, products that contain carnauba wax are preferred, mainly because carnauba is the most durable wax. Stay away from waxes or polishes that contain silicone; their chemical bonding with the paint will make paint touch-up nearly impossible. And don't fall for the claim that you only have to wax your car once a year. A good carnauba wax will protect a car that's driven daily for about three to four months.

How often should you wax? It all depends on weather conditions and how the wax is holding up. If water still beads then there is still wax on the paint. You should wax your car at least four times a year and use a cleaner wax at least once a year to remove old wax buildup. Some enthusiasts wax every month; there is a noticeable difference in doing so, because the paint develops a deeper, richer, shinier look.

WAXING PROCEDURE

How you apply the wax or polish can make a big difference in how your car will look. Some waxes come with a small applicator pad. Don't use it, because it will grab and hold any grit or dirt that was left behind by previous polishing operations. This is especially true if you've previously used a rubbing compound, which contains abrasive particles, on the car. Instead, use soft cotton diapers or plenty of soft cotton towels. Don't crumple them up in a wad; a crumpled wad will have sections that don't have any wax on them, which can scratch the paint. Also remove any rings or other jewelry and take care not to get too close to the car with beltbuckles or zippers.

Wrap the towel around two fingers, apply some wax on it and work it into a small area. It is best to wax and then buff one small area at a time. Always apply the wax on the cloth and not on the paint, and always use the minimum amount that is necessary, using a tight, circular motion to rub it into the car.

Heavy applications of wax will leave streaks and clog your towel. Once saturated with wax residue, the towel won't buff properly, and a heavy coat is much harder to buff off. If you feel you need a heavy coat of wax, it is best to apply two light coats instead of a single heavy one. Set your buffer at a slow rpm and don't use any extra pressure as you are buffing the two coats. Just use a small amount of wax, and rub it in well, reducing pressure as the wax begins to dry. If this is done correctly, the dried wax will hardly be noticeable and the residue will easily come off when you buff it out.

Applying too much wax will cause it to dry in cracks and crevices and take extra time and effort to remove later. A soft detailing brush or toothbrushes are effective tools for removing wax from crevices. Once the wax has dried, you can use a fresh clean cloth or cotton towel to buff the car's finish to a fine luster.

After waxing, wipe down the car with a damp cotton terrycloth towel or a soft brush like the Car Duster to remove any accumulated dust.

BUFFERS

Here's a cautionary word about the use of buffers on original or classic car paint. Using a buffer speeds up any polishing process, but it can very easily ruin an otherwise good painted surface. Vigorously pressing down while you're buffing can result in inadvertent "burning," or removal of the car's paint. It pays to be careful, because a vintage car with original paint that is in relatively good condition has greater potential as a collectible than one repainted due to mistakes made while buffing. Use a buffer with slow rpms and don't put any pressure on the buffer—let the buffer do the work. Gently and slowly glide the buffer along the paint surface, and don't linger on sharp corners or curves.

SANDPAPER

Some people use a very fine wet/dry sandpaper to smooth the paint and remove orange peel and other surface imperfections. Sanding takes a lot of paint off, so it is easy to get down to the primer. If the paint is badly oxidized, use polishing compound to remove the top layer. Remember that even rubbing compound won't restore dead paint.

OTHER EXTERIOR DETAILS

Windows

Clean windows are just as important as gleaming paint. Veteran concours participants use water mixed with a little ammonia and newspapers to clean window glass. It isn't the paper itself that polishes, but rather the ink which acts as a fine abrasive. After cleaning, use a product like Windex, as a polish.

For plastic rear windows on convertibles, Meguiar's, offers a 2-step plastic window polish and cleaner that removes fogging and scratches, and restores plastic windows to likenew condition.

For windshields that are scratched or pitted there are glass polishing kits available from The Eastwood Company, (www.eastwoodco.com). These kits contain special glass polishing compounds and a polishing wheel that can be used with a standard drill to remove light scratches, wiper haze, and sand sparkle.

Chrome

Chrome and bright trim can be polished and waxed. You may want to replace severely pitted trim and emblems with new ones, as they will be a blemish on an otherwise cleanly detailed car. Painted emblems should also be touched up.

Rubber and Vinyl

Rubber and vinyl should first be thoroughly cleaned. Murphy's Oil Soap is very good for this. You may want to repeat the cleaning process on these because they tend to hold dirt. After they are dry, spray with Armor All, STP Son of a Gun, or Meguiar's Intensive Protectant, letting it soak in. Follow the instructions on the product. Armor All is water based; applying it without buffing off the excess can do more harm than good. Also, putting more on won't make the surfaces glossier. If the glossy look turns you off, then give Meguiar's Intensive Protectant a try. It offers similar reconditioning and protectant qualities without the shiny finish.

Vinyl and convertible tops require extra effort. Vinyl tops are very porous and prone to trapping dirt. Start by using dish detergent and scrub with a brush, or you can use a special product such as Turtle Wax Vinyl Top Cleaner. Stubborn cases may require the use of a cleanser such as Soft Scrub. A vinyl top dressing must be used after the cleaning process to protect it; otherwise the vinyl will fade. However, don't use a protectant like Armor All; the top will be patchy, with some areas flat and others glossy. Get a special vinyl conditioner made for vinyl tops.

On the other hand, if the vinyl is severely faded, ripped, torn, or scratched, it may be more cost- and time-effective to have a new vinyl or convertible top installed. A brand-new top will look good and be much easier to maintain. Another advantage here is that taking the old top off will give you the opportunity to check for and repair any rust damage that may be present underneath.

Wheels and Tires

It has been said that wheels and tires can make or break a car. They have to be as clean and detailed as everything else. In fact, a nice set of wheels and tires on a so-so car can bring the car up more than anything else. Wheels and tires are also one of the hardest areas to keep clean.

Detailing Wheels. The best way to clean the wheels is to remove them first from the car. Start by using dish detergent and warm water on the wheels and tires. Stubborn deposits may require the use of chemical wheel cleaners such as those made by Eagle One or Mother's,. Use a stiff nylon bristle brush to scrub the tire sidewalls and tread.

Wheels can make or break your car, and it's true for your Mustang, too. Tires can be revitalized with specially made tire cleaners, such as those from Eagle One or Meguiar's. Westley's Bleche-Wite will clean the lettering on the tires superbly.

Painted wheels can be cleaned and repainted. Always use paint on wheels because it is stronger than lacquer and won't require any buffing. Another popular, although expensive, option is to have the wheels powder-coated. This is a process where the paint is baked onto the wheel. Metal hubcaps should be cleaned and polished (and sometimes painted) like any other bright work.

Finally, if your car has styled steel factory or aluminum wheels, invest in a new set of chrome lug nuts, center caps, and trim rings if the existing ones are damaged, pitted, or rusted. Small details like these can be the difference between winning first and second place in car shows.

Detailing Tires. Whitewalls and raised white letters can be rejuvenated by a whitewall cleaner, such as Westley's Bleche-White. Follow directions closely, and don't allow any of the cleaner to dry on any other part of the wheel surface as this may stain it. The rest of the tire should then be cleaned and soaked with a protectant, such as Armor All, or Eagle One's Tire Cleaner, for several hours. If you don't like the glossy, freshly dressed look, wash the tires with mild soap and water, and coat the tires with Meguiar's Intensive Protectant. Be forewarned that Armor All and other protectants will not last long in rain and will require frequent applications to maintain the new tire look. There are plenty of other cleaners available which have varying degrees of shine and are supposed to last longer, as well.

UNDERBODY

Unless you are doing a ground-up restoration, you can only do so much when it comes to the underbody of your car. Some areas are easy to get to, such as wheel wells. To get these clean, remove the wheels and flush the wheel wells with a hose, forcing out as much dirt as possible. After they are dry, you can decide whether you want to repaint the area or undercoat it. Repainting is your best bet for a car you hope to bring to a show level restoration. Undercoating would be more useful for a Mustang that has obvious blemishes to hide.

You may also find it necessary to remove any wheel well moldings in order to remove dirt from there. Use brushes to remove heavily caked-on dirt and plenty of dish detergent and water to get the area as clean as possible. Kerosene can also be used to remove heavy deposits of dirt and grime. If you have access to compressed air, use it to force dirt and water out of chassis drain holes.

Undercoating

Cars that have been undercoated present you with two choices. You can flush the underbody area, get it as clean as possible, and apply a fresh coat; or you can remove the undercoating with kerosene. It's a dirty, time-consuming job that will require hours on your back. If you take this route, wear old clothes and eye protection, because dirt and undercoating will rain down on you.

To do a proper underbody job, the rear axle, springs, shocks, gas tank, and exhaust system should be removed and detailed separately. The unibody construction of all Mustangs means that there is no separate chassis. The suspension components are bolted directly onto the body structure or subframe, so they can be removed separately. Obviously, detailing the underbody is going to be much easier if done during the restoration.

INTERIOR

Thoroughly cleaning and detailing the interior will be a lot easier if you first remove the seats. This may not be as hard as it sounds. On some cars, it will simply be a matter of loosening a few nuts and then sliding the seat out. On other cars, the nuts may be accessible from the bottom of the car.

Carpet

At this point, it's a good idea to remove the floor scuff plates that usually hold the carpets down, so you can take a look underneath the carpets. Moisture underneath the carpets is a bad sign. Check for any rust and water leaks. If the carpets are in borderline to poor condition, it might be best to replace them. Also inspect the carpeting under the foot wells for signs of water stains, since water damage here could mean there's leaking from the windshield.

Cleaning

If the carpets are stained and dirty but not worn, the first step in rejuvenating them is to thoroughly vacuum to remove all loose dirt. Then use a heavy-duty carpet shampoo to clean the carpets. Never shampoo the carpets outside of the car, as they can shrink and won't fit when reinstalled. If the lower door panels are also covered with carpeting, shampoo them as well. Don't use too much water, only just enough to keep the shampoo wet. Allow the shampoo to dry and then vacuum thoroughly once again.

Cloth, Leather, and Vinyl

To clean cloth and vinyl, start from the back and work your way forward, using an upholstery cleaner to clean any cloth-covered areas, including the headliner. A cloth headliner is like a sponge when it comes to smoke, and several applications may be required to

This is an example of a flawless interior. This 1965 Shelby interior is pretty much perfect.

225

remove stains and odors. In fact, cleaning an interior that was subject to persistent cigarette smoke will require extra effort because it penetrates everything. Work carefully as you clean the headliner; on older cars the fabric can weaken and tear if scrubbed too hard.

Vinyl-covered interior surfaces and seats can be cleaned with dish detergent and water (used sparingly) or you can use one of the many vinyl cleaners offered such as Turtle Wax Vinyl-Fabric Upholstery cleaner and protectant. Don't use soap and water or any other cleaner on leather; try a damp cloth first. On really dirty leather, use Lexol Leather Cleaner, followed by Lexol Leather Conditioner and Preservative. Meguiar's Medallion for All Leather is also excellent.

Dash Panel

To clean the dash panel, first remove all knobs. You may also want to remove the radio and any other subassembly just to make it easier to clean them. On metal dashes, use a sealer and glaze. Badly scratched metal will require reconditioning and repainting. Vinyl-covered dashes can be cleaned as described earlier. If the plastic instrument lenses are lightly scratched, use Meguiar's, two-step plastic polish to remove scratches. If the lenses are badly clouded or scratched, replace them with new units. Many times, you'll find that painted interior parts, such as knobs, levers, and the like, will show so much wear that there is no more paint on them, exposing bare plastic or metal. In this case, you may be better off repainting, replating, or replacing them all in order to maintain a uniform appearance.

After cleaning, all vinyl and plastic trim should be sprayed with Armor All or Meguiar's Intensive Protectant. Remember that protectants like Armor All are water-based, so make sure you buff off all excess. Metal and plated interior trim should be polished and waxed; badly pitted trim should be sent out for rechroming. If you decide to rechrome the interior trim, remove and send all of it out for replating at one time in order to maintain a uniform look. You'll find that most rechroming services advertise in *Hemmings Motor News*.

The Trunk

One of the most overlooked areas is the trunk. After a thorough cleaning you'll be able to tell if it needs to be repainted. Many trunks are sprayed with spatter-type paint, while others are painted the same as the body color. If equipped with a rubber trunk floor mat, there may be surface rust under the mat that will have to be removed. Check for water stains or flakes of rust because that's a tipoff to a leaking rear window. Depending on condition, you may also have to replace any trunk mats. On some cars, such as 1965–70 Mustangs, the trunk floor is formed by the top of the gas tank. It may be easier to remove the tank to get to any hidden dirt or rust trapped where the tank meets the body.

Paint and detail the jack assembly. Clean and detail the jack if damaged. Make sure the jacking instruction label is replaced with a correct reproduction. Check the lamp harness for splices or frayed wiring.

ENGINE COMPARTMENT

It is the engine that makes many of the best Mustangs unique, and the Boss 429 is a prime example. With special engine cars, the bulk of a full-blown restoration will consist of detailing the engine and engine compartment. This means, for example, unbolting everything from the firewall and inner fenders and repainting the compartment with the correct semi-gloss black paint. A properly restored Mustang will not be considered correct unless the engine compartment is restored to this original black color.

Cleaning

If you don't plan on pulling the car apart but want to detail the engine and engine compartment, you can still do a reasonably good job. The first step is to clean the engine compartment thoroughly. One of the best places to clean your engine is at a do-it-yourself hand car wash that has pressurized hoses.

Make sure the engine is fully warmed up, and seal the distributor and carburetor to prevent any water from making the engine difficult to restart later. Use a clear plastic wrap around the units to seal them. Use a spray degreaser, such as Gunk,, and spray liberally on the engine and the engine compartment, taking care not to spray on the exterior paint. You'll want to scrape off any heavy deposits of grease and grime. Let the degreaser work for several minutes and then hit it with the pressure wash. Depending on how dirty the engine is, you may have to repeat this process several times. Be prepared to have to dry out the inside of the distributor cap to get the car started again. You'll be surprised how clean the engine and engine compartment will be after several applications.

Components that can be removed and detailed outside the engine compartment will be easier to clean, and their removal will expose hard-to-reach areas. For example, removal of the alternator, power steering pump, fan, and pulleys makes them easier to clean and paint, and allows you to access those areas of the engine hidden by these components. Removing the radiator makes the front of the engine more accessible as well, plus the radiator must be cleaned, the fins straightened, and the assembly repainted. Remove the battery tray, and if heavily corroded, replace with a new one. Clean the battery and dress the terminals. Clean the cables and inspect for wear. Older cars used spring-type clamps. These are available from several reproduction sources that advertise in *Hemmings Motor News* or on the Internet.

Painting

Painting the engine and engine compartment while it is in the car is difficult at best so take the engine out if possible. If your engine's paint looks ok, just touch up damaged areas. Use a small brush to get to hard-to-reach spots. Remove any overspray with lacquer thinner.

Cables and Hoses

If the degreaser didn't remove all the grease on wiring harnesses, use lacquer thinner to clean them. This is also a good time to inspect the harness for frayed wires and damaged wrapping. Most car makers used PVC tape to wrap harnesses. You can get tape at any hardware or electrical supply store. Unwrap the harness, repair any damaged wires, and then rewrap the harness. Spark plug wires and the distributor should be removed and checked. If necessary, replace with either reproductions or correct service replacement units. The same goes for the upper and lower radiator hoses and the heater hoses. If they are soft, replace them with either reproductions or correct service replacements. Never use flexible radiator hoses, only correctly molded upper and lower radiator hoses. Also inspect the belts for wear and replace as necessary.

With many Mustangs, it is the engine that makes it unique. Extra care should be taken to detail the car's strongest asset.

At this point you also have to decide how you want the engine to look after it is detailed. Some want to preserve factory check marks, stickers, stampings, and the like as a measure of originality. Make notes of specific markings and codes, and reproduce these once the engine is painted. Also replace any original stickers and decals with reproductions. While refurbishing your engine in this fashion won't be good enough for a concours show, you'll be surprised how well your car can do at smaller, local shows where point judging is not done and absolute cleanliness and correctness is not as critical. Please refer to photos showing typical examples of engines restored to original factory specs.

Make sure the inner fenders and firewall are finished correctly to the original semi-gloss black. Bare metal parts can be polished while painted surfaces should be waxed with a one-step cleaner and wax.

HOOD

It is usually necessary to give some attention to the underside of the hood. Some cars have a hood pad designed to absorb noise and heat. It also winds up absorbing dirt. It may not be possible to clean it without ruining it. Reproduction hood pads and pad clips are available for many cars. If a reproduction is not offered and you cannot find a pad similar to yours that you can cut to fit, then refinish the underside of the hood in body color or semi-gloss, whichever is correct for your car according to the options list.

Appendix 1
Ford Production Numbers

WARRANTY PLATES AND CERTIFICATION LABELS

There were three different warranty plates used on the 1965–69 Mustangs; however, they all displayed the same information. The warranty number was the same as the Mustang's VIN. The rest of the codes indicated the body style, color code, trim code, date built code, District Sales Office (DSO), axle code, and transmission codes. If the color code was missing, that indicated that the Mustang came with a special order non-stock color.

From 1970–78, a label replaced the metal plate. The only major difference was that the month and year were shown rather than the day and month of the build date.

In 1979–80, the label was again revised to include additional information such as the air conditioning code, vinyl roof color code, and weight. In addition to the build date, a schedule date was included that showed the date and month of assembly.

The label was also changed slightly in 1981–2006 to include information about the suspension, sunroof and moonroof, and bodyside molding codes.

FORD PART NUMBERS

Ford engineering, service, and casting numbers are all deciphered in the same fashion. There are three basic groups: the prefix, basic part number, and suffix. We'll use the following number as an example:

C50E – 9425 – E

The four-digit prefix tells you the decade and year the part was released for production, the car line it was released for, and the engineering division that released it. **C** stands for the decade, in this case the 1960s. **D** would be for the 1970s, **E** for the 1980s, and so on. The next number **5** is the year—in this case, 1965. Next is **0** for the car line, and **E** for the engineering division.

The basic part number is the four-digit number in the middle. It identifies what the part is—for example, a cylinder block, carburetor, or distributor. In our example above, **9425** stands for the intake manifold. This four-digit number can include a fifth character, as in the case of distributors, where it might appear as 12 127, for instance. With some components, the basic part number doesn't appear, so the part number would appear **C5AE-A**, for the sake of space. This might happen when a tag has the part number on it, rather than the number appearing on the part itself. Carburetors will frequently have this type of abbreviated number.

Finally, there's the suffix, which is a letter code that indicates the *change level* of a given part. **A** means the original level, **B** means a second revision, and so forth. The *Ford Master Parts Catalog* has all of the details.

Obviously, the parts might look the same but the coding on them indicates what change level they really are. Individual parts also have additional numbers cast and stamped onto them independently of the code number.

CASTING DATES AND MANUFACTURING DATES

All Mustang parts have date codes that are either cast or stamped (or both) on each part. Date codes that are cast on the part indicate the date the part was cast. Manufacture dates are stamped on the metal or inked onto the part. These date codes are fairly simple to decipher. For example, if a part has the date **9 B 16**, it can be understood as follows:

9—year (1969)

B—month (February)

16—day of the month

Most Mustang parts were cast or manufactured before each car was actually built. This resulted in date codes that sometimes preceded vehicle manufacture dates by as much as thirty days. Discrepancies in casting dates for parts and model manufacture dates could bring into question a Mustang's claim to original or stock status. So it is wise to cross-reference.

Mustangs built from 1979 on have a much shorter time between casting manufacture and final vehicle assembly because Ford went to a just-in-time production schedule.

Sheet Metal Date Codes

In much the same way, Mustang sheet metal was stamped to show the date it was manufactured. For example, a sheet metal part with **10 5 D 1** is broken down as follows:

10—month (October)

5—day of the month

D—stamping plant (Dearborn)

1—shift (first shift)

Although sheet metal date codes do not indicate the year of manufacture, as other components do, the stamping date will fall up to 30 days before the vehicle manufacture date. Third and later generation Mustang sheet metal is dated the same way. However, replacement sheet metal will also have a month and year code, such as **9 85** (September 1985), preceding the regular date code.

Appendix 2
Ford VIN Decoder

The following VIN decoder is applicable to all Mustangs.

Previous to 1970, a warranty plate was attached on the driver's door. From 1970-on, the location of the plate has remained on the driver's side of the instrument panel, and a certification label has been attached to the rear face of the driver's door.

1965

Serial Numbers

5F07F100001

5—Last digit of model year

F—Assembly plant (F—Dearborn, R—San Jose, T—Metuchen)

07—Plate code for 2dr Mustang (08—convertible, 09—fastback)

F—Engine code

100001—Consecutive unit number

Location

Stamped on the driver's side inner fender panel, at the notch in the fender between the shock tower and radiator support. Warranty plate is riveted on the rear face of the driver's door.

Engine Codes

U—170 ci 1V 6 cyl 101hp (early 1965)

T—200 ci 1V 6 cyl 120hp

F—260 ci 2V V-8 164hp (early 1965)

C—289 ci 2V V-8 200hp

D—289 ci 4V V-8 210hp (early 1965)

A—289 ci 4V V-8 225hp

K—289 ci 4V V-8 271hp High Performance

Serial Numbers

Shelby VIN

SFM5S001

SFM—Shelby Ford Mustang

5—Model year (1965)

S—Street (R—Race)

001—Consecutive production number (001 to 562)

Location

On the pop-riveted plate on the driver's side inner fender panel over the Ford VIN. Also stamped on the passenger's side inner fender panel, halfway between the firewall and the radiator.

Ford VIN

5R09K000001

5—Last digit of model year

R—Assembly plant (R—San Jose)

09—Body code (09—2dr fastback)

K—Engine code (271hp 289 ci V-8)

000001—Consecutive unit number

Location

Underneath the Shelby VIN plate. On the driver's and passenger's side inner fender panels at outside edge near shock tower. Can only be viewed if fenders are removed. On original engine block, beneath front exhaust port on passenger side.

Engine Code

K—289 ci V-8 306hp

1966

Serial Numbers

6F07C100001
6—Last digit of model year
F—Assembly plant (F—Dearborn, R—San Jose, T—Metuchen)
07—Plate code for 2dr Mustang (08—convertible, 09—fastback)
C—Engine code
100001—Consecutive unit number

Location

Stamped on the driver's side inner fender panel, at the notch between the shock tower and radiator support. Warranty plate is riveted on the rear face of the driver's door.

Engine Codes

T—200 ci 1V 6 cyl 120hp
C—289 ci 2V V-8 200hp
A—289 ci 4V V-8 225hp
K—289 ci 4V V-8 271hp

Serial Numbers

Shelby VIN

SFM6S0001
SFM—Shelby Ford Mustang
6—Last digit of model year
S—Street
0001—Consecutive unit number (0001 to 2380)

Location

On plate pop-riveted on the driver's side inner fender panel covering.

Ford VIN

Also on the passenger's side inner front fender panel halfway between radiator and firewall.

Ford VIN

6R09K000001

6—Last digit of model year
R—Assembly plant (R—San Jose)
09—Body code (09—Mustang 2dr 2+2)
K—Engine code, 271hp 289 ci
000001—Ford consecutive production number

Engine Code
K—289 ci V-8 306hp

1967

Serial Numbers
7R01C100001
7—Last digit of model year
R—Assembly plant (F—Dearborn, R—San Jose, T—Metuchen)
01—Plate code for 2dr hardtop (02—fastback, 03—convertible)
C—Engine code
100001—Consecutive unit number

Location
Stamped on the driver's side inner fender panel, at the notch between the shock tower and radiator support. Warranty plate is riveted on the rear face of the driver's door.

Engine Codes
U—200 ci 1V 6 cyl 120hp
C—289 ci 2V V-8 200hp
A—289 ci 4V V-8 225hp
K—289 ci 4V V-8 271hp
S—390 ci 4V V-8 320hp

Shelby Serial Numbers
67200F2A000000
67—Model year
2—Engine (2—289, 4—428)
0—Transmission (0—4-speed, 1—automatic)
0—Base vehicle component (0—base vehicle, 1—Ford air conditioning, 2—Thermactor exhaust

emission, 3—air conditioning and Thermactor exhaust)

F—Body code (F—fastback)

2—Exterior color code

A—Interior trim

000000—Consecutive Shelby production number (00001 to 3225)

Location

Stamped plate is pop-riveted on the driver's side inner front fender panel, over the Ford VIN. VIN is also stamped on the passenger's side inner fender panel, halfway between the firewall and radiator.

Ford VIN

7R02K00001

7—Last digit of model year

R—Assembly plant (R—San Jose)

02—Body code (02—2dr fastback)

K—Engine code (K—271hp 289 ci, Q—428 ci)

00001—Consecutive Ford production number

Location

Stamped on the driver's side fender panel, underneath the Shelby VIN plate. Stamped on the passenger's and driver's side inner front fender panel near the outside edge of the shock tower. Visible only when the fender is removed. On some GT350s, it is stamped on the engine block beneath the front exhaust port on the passenger's side. On four-speed cars, it is stamped on the transmission case.

Engine Codes

K—289 ci V-8 306hp

Q—428 ci V-8 355hp

1968

Serial Numbers

8R01J100001

8—Last digit of model year

R—Assembly plant (F—Dearborn, R—San Jose, T—Metuchen)

01—Plate code for 2dr hardtop (02—fastback, 03—convertible)
J—Engine code
100001—Consecutive unit number

Location
Stamped on plate riveted on the passenger's side of the instrument panel, visible through the windshield. Warranty plate is riveted on the rear face of the driver's door.

Engine Codes
T—200 ci 1V 6 cyl 120hp
C—289 ci 2V V-8 195hp
F—302 ci 2V V-8 210hp
J—302 ci 4V V-8 230hp
X– 390 ci 2V V-8 295hp
S—390 ci 4V V-8 325hp
W—427 ci 4V V-8 390hp
R—428 ci 4V V-8 335hp (Cobra Jet)

Shelby VIN
8T02J000001-00001
8—Last digit of model year
T—Assembly plant (T—Metuchen)
02—Body code (02—fastback, 03—convertible)
J—Engine code (J—302, S—428, R—428CJ-R)
000001—Consecutive Ford production number
00001—Consecutive Shelby production number (00001 to 04450)

Location
Stamped on plate which is pop-riveted on the driver's side inner front fender panel over the Ford VIN.

Ford VIN
Exactly the same as the Shelby VIN but without the consecutive Shelby production number.

Location
Stamped on the driver's side inner fender panel, underneath the Shelby VIN plate. Stamped on plate riveted on the instrument panel on the passenger side; visible through the windshield.

Stamped on the warranty plate on the driver's door rear face; the plate also reads, "Special Performance Vehicle."

Engine Codes
J—302 ci V-8 250hp
S—428 ci V-8 360hp
R—428 ci V-8 335hp (CJ)

1969

Serial Numbers
9F02Z100001
9—Last digit of model year
F—Assembly plant (F—Dearborn, R—San Jose, T—Metuchen)
02—Plate code for Mustang fastback (01—hardtop, 03— convertible)
Z—Engine code
100001—Consecutive unit number

Location
Stamped on plate riveted on the driver's side of instrument panel, visible through the windshield. Warranty plate is riveted on the rear face of the driver's door.

Engine Codes
T—200 ci 1V 6 cyl 115hp
L—250 ci 1V 6 cyl 155hp
F—302 ci 2V V-8 220hp
G—302 ci 4V V-8 (Boss) 290hp
H—351 ci 2V V-8 250hp
M—351 ci 4V V-8 290hp
S—390 ci 4V V-8 320hp
Q—428 ci 4V V-8 (CJ) 335hp
R—428 ci 4V V-8 (CJ-R) 335hp
Z—429 ci 4V V-8 (Boss) 375hp

Shelby VIN (includes 1970 model year)
9F02M480001

9—Last digit of model year (0—1970 updated cars)
F—Assembly plant (F—Dearborn)
M—Engine code (M—351, R—428CJ-R)
48—Shelby code
0001—Consecutive production number

Location

Plate riveted to the dash panel on the driver's side, visible through windshield. Stamped on the warranty plate located on the face of the driver's door. Plate also reads "Special Performance Vehicle." Stamped on the driver's and passenger's inner fender panel halfway between the shock tower and firewall. Visible with fenders removed. Additional plate stating "Custom-Crafted by Shelby Automotive, Inc." is attached above warranty plate.

Engine Codes

M—351 ci 4V V-8 290hp
R—428 ci 4V V-8 335hp (CJ)

1970

Serial Numbers

0F04F100001
0—Last digit of model year
F—Assembly plant code (F—Dearborn, R—San Jose, T—Metuchen)
04—Plate code for Mustang (01—Hardtop, 02—Fastback, 03— convertible, 04—Grande, 05—Mach 1)
F—Engine code
100001—Consecutive unit number

Location

Stamped on plate riveted to the instrument panel on the driver's side, visible through the windshield. A vehicle certification label replaced the previous warranty plate. It was mounted on the rear face of the driver's door.

Engine Codes

T—200 ci 1V 6 cyl 120hp
L—250 ci 1V 6 cyl 155hp

F—302 ci 2V V-8 220hp

G—302 ci 4V V-8 290hp (Boss)

H—351 ci 2V V-8 250hp (351W & 351C)

M—351 ci 4V V-8 300hp

Q—428 ci 4V V-8 335hp (Cobra Jet)

R—428 ci 4V V-8 335hp (Cobra Jet Ram Air)

Z—429 ci 4V V-8 375hp (Boss)

1971

Serial Numbers

1F01M100001

1—Last digit of model year

F—Assembly plant (F—Dearborn, R—San Jose, T—Metuchen)

01—Plate code for Mustang body (01—2dr hardtop, 02—2dr SportsRoof, 03—convertible, 04—2dr hardtop Grande, 05—2dr SportsRoof Mach 1)

M—Engine code

100001—Consecutive unit number

Location

Stamped on plate attached to the driver's side of the instrument panel, visible through the windshield. Certification label is attached to the rear face of the driver's door.

Engine Codes

L—250 ci 1V 6 cyl 145hp

F—302 ci 2V V-8 210hp

H—351 ci 2V V-8 240hp

M—351 ci 4V V-8 280hp (CJ)

M—351 ci 4V V-8 285hp

R—351 ci 4V V-8 330hp (Boss)

C—429 ci 4V V-8 370hp (CJ)

J—429 ci 4V V-8 375hp (CJ-R)

1972

Serial Numbers

2F05Q100001

2—Last digit of model year

F—Assembly plant (F—Dearborn)

05—Plate code for Mustang (01—2dr hardtop, 02—2dr SportsRoof, 03—convertible, 04—2dr hardtop Grande, 05—2dr SportsRoof Mach 1)

Q—Engine code

100001—Consecutive unit number

Engine Codes

L—250 ci 1V 6 cyl 98hp

F—302 ci 2V V-8 140hp

H—351 ci 2V V-8 177hp

Q—351 ci 4V V-8 266hp(CJ)

R—351 ci 4V V-8 275 hp(HO)

1973

Serial Numbers

3R03H100001

3—Last digit of model year

R—Assembly plant (F—Dearborn, R—San Jose, T—Metuchen)

03—Plate code for Mustang (01—2dr hardtop, 02—2dr SportsRoof, 03—convertible, 04—2dr hardtop Grande, 05—2dr SportsRoof—Mach 1)

H—Engine code

100001—Consecutive unit number

Engine Codes

L—250 ci 1V 6 cyl 99hp

F—302 ci 2V V-8 141hp

H—351 ci 2V V-8 177hp

Q—351 ci 4V V-8 266hp (CJ)

1974

Serial numbers

4R02Y100001

4—Last digit of model year

R—Assembly plant (F—Dearborn, R—San Jose, T—Metuchen)

02—Plate code for Mustang (02—2dr hardtop, 03—3dr hatchback, 04—2dr hardtop Ghia, 05—3dr hatchback Mach 1)

Y—Engine code

100001—Consecutive unit number

Engine codes

Y—140 ci 2.3L 2V 4 cyl 88hp

Z—171 ci 2.8L 2V V-6 105hp

1975

Serial Numbers

5F03Y100001

5—Last digit of model year

F—Assembly plant (F—Dearborn, R—San Jose, T—Metuchen)

03—Plate code for Mustang (02—2dr hardtop, 03—3dr hatchback, 04—2dr hardtop Ghia, 05—3dr hatchback Mach 1)

Y– Engine code

100001—Consecutive unit number

Engine Codes

Y—140 ci 2.3l 2V 4 cyl 88hp

Z—171 ci 2.8l 2V V6 105hp

F—302 ci 5.0l 2V V8 140hp

1976

Serial Numbers

6F03Y100001

6—Last digit of model year
F—Assembly plant (F—Dearborn, R—San Jose)
03—Plate code for Mustang (02—2dr hardtop, 03—3dr hatchback, 04—2dr hardtop Ghia, 05—3dr hatchback Mach 1)
Y—Engine code
100001—Consecutive unit number

Engine Codes
Y—140 ci 2.3l 2V 4 cyl 88hp
Z—171 ci 2.8l 2V V6 105hp
F—302 ci 5.0l 2V V8 140hp

1977

Serial Numbers
7F03Y100001
7—Last digit of model year
F—Assembly plant (F—Dearborn, R—San Jose)
03—Plate code for Mustang (02—2dr Hardtop, 03—3dr Hatchback, 04—2dr Hardtop Ghia, 05—3dr Hatchback Mach 1)
Y—Engine code
100001—Consecutive unit number

Engine Codes
Y—140 ci 2.3l 2V 4 cyl 92hp
Z—171 ci 2.8l 2V V6 103hp
F—302 ci 5.0l 2V V8 134hp

1978

Serial Numbers
8F03Y100001
8—Last digit of model year
F—Assembly plant (F—Dearborn, R—San Jose)
03—Plate code for Mustang (02—2dr hardtop, 03—3dr hatchback, 04—2dr hardtop Ghia, 05—

3dr hatchback Mach 1)
Y—Engine code
100001—Consecutive unit number

Engine Codes

Y—140 ci 2.3l 2V 4 cyl 88hp
Z—171 ci 2.8l 2V V6 90hp
F—302 ci 5.0l 2V V8 139hp

1979

Serial Numbers

9F02Y100001
9—Last digit of model year
F—Assembly plant (F—Dearborn, R—San Jose)
02—Plate code for Mustang (02—2dr sedan, 03—3dr hatchback, 04—2dr Ghia, 05—3dr Ghia)
Y—Engine code
100001—Consecutive unit number

Engine Codes

Y—2.3l 2V 4 cyl 88hp
W—2.3l 2V 4 cyl 132hp (Turbocharged)
Z—2.8l 2V V6 109hp
T—3.3l 1V hp 85hp

Serial Numbers

1FABP10A6BF000001
1FA—Ford Motor Co.
B—Indicates restraint system (B—Active Belts)
P—Passenger car
10—Body code (10/14H—2dr sedan, 15—3dr, 12—2dr Ghia, 13—3dr Ghia)
A—Engine code
6—Check digit, which varies
B—Year (B—1981)
F—Plant (F—Dearborn)
000001—Consecutive unit number

Engine Codes
A—2.3l 2V 4 cyl 88hp
B—3.3l 1V 6 cyl 94hp
D—4.2l 2V V-8 120hp
F—5.0l 2V V8 140hp

1980

Serial Numbers
0F02A100001
0—Last digit of model year
F—Assembly plant (F—Dearborn, R—San Jose)
02—Plate code for Mustang (02—2dr sedan, 03—3dr hatchback, 04—2dr Ghia, 05—3dr Ghia)
A—Engine code
100001—Consecutive unit number

Engine Codes
A—2.3l 2V 4 cyl 88hp(MT), 90hp(AT)
W—2.3l 2V 4 cyl (Turbocharged)
B—3.3l 1V 6 cyl 91hp(MT), 94hp(AT)
D—4.2l 2V V8 119hp

1981

Serial Numbers
1FABP10A6BF000001
1FA—Ford Motor Co.
B—Indicates restraint system (B—Active belts)
P—Passenger car
10—Body code (10/14H—2dr sedan, 15—3dr, 12—2dr Ghia, 13—3dr Ghia)
A—Engine code
6—Check digit, which varies
B—Year (B—1981)
F—Plant (F—Dearborn)
000001—Consecutive unit number

Engine Codes

A—2.3l 2V 4 cyl 88hp
B—3.3l 1V 6 cyl 94hp
D—4.2l 2V V-8 120hp

1982

Serial Numbers

1FABP10A6CF000001
1FA—Ford Motor Co.
B—Restraint system (B—Active belts)
P—Passenger car
10—Body code (10—2dr L/GL, 16—3dr GL/GT, 12—2dr GLX, 13—3dr GLX)
A—Engine code
6—Check digit, which varies
C—Year (C—1982)
F—Plant (F—Dearborn)
000001—Consecutive unit number

Engine Codes

A—2.3l 2V 4 cyl 88hp
B—3.3l 1V 6 cyl 94hp
D—4.2l 2V V-8 120hp
F—5.0l 2V V-8 157hp

1983

Serial Numbers

1FABP26A6DF000001
1FA—Ford Motor Co.
B—Restraint system (B—Active belts)
P—Passenger car
26—Body code (26—2dr sedan, 27—2dr convertible, 28—3dr hatchback)
A—Engine code
6—Check digit, which varies

D—Model year (D—1983)
F—Assembly plant (F—Dearborn)
000001—Consecutive unit number

Engine Codes
A—2.3l 1V 4 cyl 88hp
T—2.3l EFI, 4 cyl 145hp (Turbo GT)
3—3.8l 2V V-6 112hp
F—5.0l 4V V-8 175hp HO

1984

Serial Numbers
1FABP26M6EF000001
1FA—Ford Motor Co.
B—Restraint system (B—Active belts)
P—Passenger car
26—Body code (26—2dr sedan, 27—2dr convertible, 28—3dr hatchback)
M—Engine code
6—Check digit, which varies
E—Year (E—1984)
F—Assembly plant (F—Dearborn)
000001—Consecutive unit number

Engine Codes
A—2.3l 1V 4 cyl 88hp
T—2.3l EFI 4 cyl 145hp (Turbo GT)
W—2.3l EFI 4 cyl 175hp (SVO)
3—3.8l EFI V-8 120hp
M—5.0l 4V/EFI V-8 175/165hp HO

1985

Serial Numbers
1FABP26M6FF000001
1FA—Ford Motor Co.

B—Restraint system (B—Active belts)

P—Passenger car

26—Body code (26—2dr sedan, 27—2dr convertible, 28—3dr hatchback)

M—Engine code

6—Check digit, which varies

F—Year (F—1985)

F—Assembly plant (F—Dearborn)

000001—Consecutive unit number

Engine Codes

A—2.3l 1V 4 cyl 88hp

T—2.3l EFI 4 cyl 205hp (SVO)

3—3.8l EFI V6 120hp

M—5.0l EFl/4V V8 165/210hp HO

1986

Serial Numbers

1FABP26M6GF000001

1FA—Ford Motor Co.

B—Restraint system (B—Active belts)

P—Passenger car

26—Body code (26—2dr sedan, 27—2dr convertible, 28—3dr hatchback)

M—Engine code

6—Check digit, which varies

G—Model year (G—1986)

F—Plant (F—Dearborn)

000001—Consecutive unit number

Engine Codes

A—2.3l 1V 4 cyl 88hp

T—2.3l EFI 4 cyl 200hp(SVO)

3—3.8l EFI V-6 120hp

M—5.0l EFI V-8 200hp HO

1987

Serial Numbers

1FABP40M6HF000001

1FA—Ford Motor Co.

B—Restraint system (B—Active belts)

P—Passenger car

40—Body code (40—2dr LX, 41—3dr LX, 44—2dr LX convertible, 42—3dr GT, 45—2dr GT convertible)

M—Engine code

6—Check digit, which varies

H—Year (H—1987)

F—Plant (F—Dearborn)

000001—Consecutive unit number

Engine codes

A—2.3l 1V 4 cyl 88hp

M—5.0l EFI V-8 225hp H0

1988

Serial Numbers

1FABP40E6JF000001

1FA—Ford Motor Co.

B—Restraint system (B—Active belts)

P—Passenger car

40—Body code (40—2dr LX, 41—3dr LX, 42—3dr GT, 44—2dr LX convertible, 45—2dr GT convertible)

E—Engine code

6—Check digit, which varies

J—Model year (J—1988)

F—Plant (F—Dearborn)

000001—Consecutive unit number

Engine Codes

A—2.3Ll 1V 4 cyl 88hp

E—5.0l EFI V-8 225hp HO

1989

Serial Numbers

1FABP40A6KF000001

1FA—Ford Motor Co.

B—Restraint system (B—Active belts)

P—Passenger car

40—Body code (40—2dr LX, 41—3dr LX, 42—3dr GT, 44—2dr LX convertible, 45—2dr GT convertible) ·

A—Engine code

6—Check digit, which varies

K—Model year (K—1989)

F—Assembly plant (F—Dearborn)

000001—Consecutive unit number

Engine Codes

A—2.3l 1V 4 cyl 88hp

E—5.0l EFI V-8 225hp HO

1990

Serial Numbers

1FACP40A6LF000001

1FA—Ford Motor Co.

C—Restraint system (C—Air bags & active belts)

P—Passenger car

40—Body code (40—2dr LX, 41—3dr LX, 42—3dr GT, 44—2dr convertible, 45—GT convertible)

A—Engine code

6—Check digit, which varies

L—Model year (L—1990)

F—Assembly plant (F—Dearborn)

000001—Consecutive unit number

Engine Codes

A—2.3l EFI 4 cyl 88hp

E—5.0l EFI V-8 225hp HO

1991

Serial Numbers

1FACP40E6MF000001

1FA—Ford Motor Co.

C—Restraint system (C—Air bags & active belts)

P—Passenger car

40—Body code (40—2dr LX, 41—3dr LX, 42—3dr GT, 44—2dr convertible, 45—GT convertible)

E—Engine code

6—Check digit, which varies

M—Model year (M—1991)

F—Assembly plant (F—Dearborn)

000001—Consecutive unit number

Engine Codes

A—2.3l EFI 4 cyl 105hp

E—5.0l EFI V-8 225hp HO

1992

Serial Numbers

1FACP40E6NF000001

1FA—Ford Motor Co.

C—Restraint system (C—Air bags & active belts)

P—Passenger car

40—Body code (40—2dr LX, 41—3dr LX, 42—3dr GT, 44—2dr convertible, 45—GT convertible)

E—Engine code

6—Check digit, which varies

N—Model year (N—1992)

F—Assembly plant (F—Dearborn)

000001—Consecutive unit number

Engine Codes

M—2.3l EFI 4 cyl 105hp

E—5.0l EFI V-8 225hp HO

1993

Serial Numbers

1FACP40E6PF000001

1FA—Ford Motor Co.

C—Restraint system (C—Air bags & active belts)

P—Passenger car

40—Body code (40—2dr LX, 41—3dr LX, 42—3dr GT, 44—2dr convertible, 45—GT convertible)

E—Engine code

6—Check digit, which varies

P—Model year (P—1993)

F—Assembly plant (F—Dearborn)

000001—Consecutive unit number

Engine Codes

M—2.3l EFI 4 cyl 105hp

E—5.0l EFI V-8 205hp HO

D—5.0l EFI 235hp

1994

Serial Numbers

1FALP4046RF000001

1FA—Ford Motor Co.

L—Restraint system (L—Air bags & active belts)

P—Passenger car

40—Body code (40—2dr, 42—2dr GT, 44—2dr convertible, 45—GT convertible)

4—Engine code

6—Check digit, which varies

R—Model year (R—1994)

F—Assembly plant (F—Dearborn)

000001—Consecutive unit number

Engine Codes

4—3.8l EFI V-6 145hp

E—5.0l EFI V-8 215hp
D—5.0l EFI V-8 240hp

1995

Serial Numbers

1FALP4046SF000001

1FA—Ford Motor Co.

L—Restraint system (L—Air bags & active belts)

P—Passenger car

40—Body code (40—2dr, 42—2dr GT, 44—2dr convertible, 45—GT convertible)

4—Engine code

6—Check digit, which varies

S—Model year (S—1995)

F—Assembly plant (F—Dearborn)

000001—Consecutive unit number

Engine Codes

4—3.8l EFI V-6 145hp
E—5.0l EFI V-8 215hp
D—5.0l EFI V-8 240hp
C—5.8l EFI V-8 300hp

1996

Serial Numbers

1FALP45X6TF000001

1FA—Ford Motor Co.

L—Restraint system (L—Air bags & active belts)

P—Passenger car

45—Body code (40—coupe, 42—GT coupe, 44—convertible, 45—GT convertible, 47—Cobra coupe, 46—Cobra convertible)

X—Engine code

6—Check digit, which varies

T—Model year (T—1996)

F—Assembly plant (F—Dearborn)
000001—Consecutive unit number

Engine Codes
4—3.8l EFI V-6 150hp
X—4.6l EFI V-8 215hp
V—4.6l EFI V-8 305hp SVT Cobra

1997

Serial Numbers
1FALP45X6VF000001
1FA—Ford Motor Co.
L—Restraint system (L—Air bags & active belts)
P—Passenger car
45—Body code (40—coupe, 42—GT coupe, 44—convertible, 45—GT convertible, 47—Cobra coupe, 46—Cobra convertible)
X—Engine code
6—Check digit, which varies
V—Model year (V—1997)
F—Assembly plant (F—Dearborn)
000001—Consecutive unit number

Engine Codes
4—3.8l EFI V-6 150hp
X—4.6l SOHC EFI V-8 215hp
V—4.6l DOHC EFI V-8 305hp

1998

Serial Numbers
1FALP45X6WF000001
1FA—Ford Motor Co.
L—Restraint system (L—Air bags & active belts)
P—Passenger car

45—Body code (40—coupe, 42—GT coupe, 44—convertible, 45—GT convertible, 47—Cobra coupe, 46—Cobra convertible)

X—Engine code

6—Check digit, which varies

W—Model year (W—1998)

F—Assembly plant (F—Dearborn)

000001—Consecutive unit number

Engine Codes

4—3.8l EFI V-6 150hp

X—4.6l SOHC EFI V-8 225hp

V—4.6l DOHC EFI V-8 305hp (SVT Cobra)

1999

Serial Numbers

1FALP45X6XF000001

1FA—Ford Motor Co.

L—Restraint system (L—Air bags & active belts)

P—Passenger car

45—Body code (40—coupe, 42—GT coupe, 44—convertible, 45—GT convertible, 47—Cobra coupe, 46—Cobra convertible)

X—Engine code

6—Check digit, which varies

X—Model year (X—1999)

F—Assembly plant (F—Dearborn)

000001—Consecutive unit number

Engine Codes

4—3.8l EFI V-6 190hp

X—4.6l SOHC EFI V-8 260hp

V—4.6l DOHC EFI V-8 320hp SVT Cobra

2000

Serial Numbers

1FALP45X6YF000001

1FA—Ford Motor Co.

L—Restraint system (L—Air bags & active belts)

P—Passenger car

45—Body code (40—coupe, 42—GT coupe, 44—convertible, 45—GT convertible, 47—Cobra coupe)

X—Engine code

6—Check digit, which varies

Y—Model year (Y—2000)

F—Assembly plant (F—Dearborn)

000001—Consecutive unit number

Engine Codes

4—3.8l EFI V-6 190hp

X—4.6l SOHC EFI V-8 260hp

H—5.4l SOHC EFI V-8 SVT Cobra "R"

2001

Serial Numbers

1FALP45X61F000001

1FA—Ford Motor Co.

L—Restraint system (L—Air bags & active belts)

P—Passenger car

45—Body code (40—coupe, 42—GT coupe, 44—convertible, 45—GT convertible, 47—Cobra coupe, 46—Cobra convertible)

X—Engine code

6—Check digit, which varies

1—Model year (1—2001)

F—Assembly plant (F—Dearborn)

000001—Consecutive unit number

Engine Codes
4—3.8l EFI V-6 193hp
X—4.6l SOHC EFI V-8 260hp (265hp Bullitt)
V—4.6l DOHC EFI V-8 320hp SVT Cobra

2002

Serial Numbers
1FALP45X62F000001
1FA—Ford Motor Co.
L—Restraint system (L—Air bags & active belts)
P—Passenger car
45—Body code (40—coupe, 42—GT coupe, 44—convertible, 45—GT convertible)
X—Engine code
6—Check digit, which varies
2—Model year (2—2002)
F—Assembly plant (F—Dearborn)
000001—Consecutive unit number

Engine Codes
4—3.8l EFI V-6 193hp
X—4.6l SOHC EFI V-8 260hp

2003

Serial Numbers
1FALP45X63F000001
1FA—Ford Motor Co.
L—Restraint system (L—Air bags & active belts)
P—Passenger car
45—Body code (40—coupe, 42—GT coupe, 44—convertible, 45—GT convertible, 48—Cobra coupe, 49—Cobra convertible)
X—Engine code
6—Check digit, which varies
3—Model year (3—2003)

F—Assembly plant (F—Dearborn)
000001—Consecutive unit number

Engine Codes

4—3.8l EFI V-6 190hp
X—4.6l SOHC EFI V-8 260h
R—4.6l DOHC EFI V-8 305hp Mach 1
Y—4.6l DOHC EFI V-8 S/C 390hp SVT Cobra

2004

Serial Numbers

1FALP45X64F000001
1FA—Ford Motor Co.
L—Restraint system (L—Air bags & active belts)
P—Passenger car
45—Body code (40—coupe, 42—GT coupe, 44—convertible, 45—GT convertible, 48—Cobra coupe, 49—Cobra convertible)
X—Engine code
6—Check digit, which varies
4—Model year (4—2004)
F—Assembly plant (F—Dearborn)
000001—Consecutive unit number

Engine Codes

4—3.8l EFI V-6 193hp
6—3.9l EFI V-6
R—4.6l SOHC EFI V-8 260hp
X—4.6l DOHC EFI V-8 310hp Mach 1 (308hp automatic)
Y—4.6l DOHC EFI V-8 S/C 390hp SVT Cobra

2005

1ZVLT80H655000001
1ZV—Ford Motor Co.

L—Restraint system (L—Air bags & active belts)

T—Passenger car

80—Body code (80—coupe, 82—GT coupe, 84—convertible, 85—GT convertible)

H—Engine code

6—Check digit, which varies

5—Model year (5—2005)

5—Assembly plant (5—Flat Rock)

000001—Consecutive unit number

Engine Codes
N—4.0l EFI SOHC V-6 210hp

H—4.6l EFI SOHC 3—valve V-8 300hp

2006

1ZVLT80H665000001

1ZV—Ford Motor Co.

L—Restraint system (L—Air bags & active belts)

T—Passenger car

80—Body code (80—coupe, 82—GT coupe, 84—convertible, 85—GT convertible)

H—Engine code

6—Check digit, which varies

6—Model year (6—2006)

5—Assembly plant (5—Flat Rock)

000001—Consecutive unit number

Engine Codes
N—4.0l EFI SOHC V-6 210hp

H—4.6l EFI SOHC 3—valve V-8 300hp

Appendix 3
Mustang Sources

CAR CLUBS

Mustang Club of America
4051 Barrancas Avenue
PMB 102
Pensacola, FL 32507
www.mustang.org

Shelby American Automobile Club
P.O. Box 788
Sharon, CT 06069
www.saac.com

INFORMATION SOURCES

Hemmings Motor News
222 Main Street
Bennington, VT 05201
www.hemmings.com

Motorbooks International Publishing, Inc.

729 Prospect Avenue

P.O. Box 1

Osceola, WI 54020

www.motorbooks.com

Mustang Monthly

P.O. Box 420698

Palm Coast, FL 32142

www.mustangmonthly.com

PART SOURCES

Auto Custom Carpets, Inc.   Automotive Carpets

P.O. Box 1350

1429 Noble Street

Anniston, AL 36201

www.accmats.com

Auto Krafters, Inc.   Mustang Parts 1964–1973

P.O. Box 1100

New Market, VA 22844

www.autokrafters.com

Tony D. Branda Shelby & Mustang Parts   Mustang and Shelby Parts 1964–1973

1434 E. Pleasant Valley Boulevard

Altoona, PA 16602

800-458-3477

CJ Pony Parts   Mustang Parts 1965–2006

7481 Allentown Boulevard

Harrisburg, PA 17112

www.cjponyparts.com

California Car Cover Company   Car Covers
9525 Desoto Avenue
Chatsworth, CA 91311
www.calcarcover.com

California Mustang Parts and Accessories   Mustang Parts 1964–2006
19400 San Jose Avenue
City of Industry, CA 91748
www.cal-mustang.com

The Eastwood Company   Tools
263 Shoemaker Road
Pottstown, PA 19464
www.eastwoodco.com

Glazier's Mustang Barn   Mustang Parts 1964–1973
531 Wambold Road
Souderton, PA 18964
www.mustangbarn.com

Larry's Thunderbird & Mustang Parts, Inc.   Mustang Parts 1965–1973
1180 California Avenue #B
Corona, CA 92881
www.larrystbird.com

Latemodel Restoration Supply   Mustang Parts 1979–2006
400 Jan Drive
Hewitt, TX 76643
www.50resto.com

Mustangs Unlimited   Mustang Parts
185 Adams Street
Manchester, CT 06042
www.mustangsunlimited.com

National Parts Depot   Mustang Parts 1965–1973
NPD Florida
900 S.W. 38th Avenue
Ocala, Fl 34474
www.nationalpartsdepot.com

The Paddock Performance & Restoration   Mustang Parts 1964–1993
7565 South State Road 109
Knightstown, IN 46148
www.paddockparts.com

Restomotive Laboratories   Rust Treatment
P.O. Box 1235
Morristown, NJ 07962
www.POR15.com

Steeda Autosports, Inc.   Mustang Parts 1979–2005
1351 NW Steeda Way
Pompano Beach, FL 33069
www.steeda.com

Universal Urethane, Inc.   Mustang Door and Dash Panels
4201 E. Lone Mountain Road
North Las Vegas, NV 89031
www.dashesdirect.com

Virginia Classic Mustang Inc.   Mustang Parts 1965–1973
195 W. Lee Street
Broadway, VA 22815
www.virginiaclassicmustang.com

Year One   Mustang Parts 1964–1973, 1979–2004
P.O. Box 521
Braselton, GA 30517
www.yearone.com

Index

Pony 9, 20, 21, 23, 28, 31, 32, 34, 52, 61, 65, 75, 81, 83, 112, 151, 179, 180, 264
power brakes 13, 19, 41, 74, 117, 132, 159, 192
power steering 13, 20, 21, 41, 42, 52, 56, 74, 93, 117, 132, 192, 194, 205, 227
pushrod 157

quarter panels 12, 27, 29, 32, 33, 79, 199

rack-and-pinion steering/system 113, 159, 194
Rally Pac 20, 21, 23, 28
Ram Air induction 40, 41
rear wing 50, 53, 62, 66, 69, 76, 85, 141, 145, 170
reupholstery 197
rev-limiter 54
rocker arms 19, 54, 63, 74, 76, 191
rod(s) 19, 42, 49, 54, 57, 58, 64, 76, 98, 108, 126, 160, 175, 179, 200

SCCA 52, 67, 90
scoops 26, 32, 33, 38, 41, 42, 43, 44, 46, 48, 49, 50, 51, 52, 53, 56, 62, 65, 66, 67, 68, 75, 90, 92, 93, 94, 96, 97, 100, 101, 104, 105, 114, 115, 116, 126, 128, 130, 139, 141, 145, 167, 168, 172, 173, 175, 177
Shaker scoop 48, 49, 172, 173
Shelby 5, 8, 34, 43, 46, 47, 51, 55, 68, 87, 88, 89, 90, 91, 92, 93, 94, 95, 96, 97, 98, 99, 100, 101, 102, 103, 104, 105, 106, 107, 108, 109, 110, 114, 115, 127, 131, 132, 177, 188, 189, 190, 206, 207, 225, 236, 237, 238, 239, 240, 241, 242, 263, 264
Shelby Mustang 5, 43, 46, 51, 55, 87, 89, 90, 91, 92, 93, 94, 95, 96, 97, 98, 99, 100, 101, 102, 103, 105, 106, 107, 109, 114, 115, 127, 189, 190
shock absorber 41, 90, 132
Shotgun 429 57
side scoops 26, 38, 43, 46, 53, 56, 62, 92, 93, 94, 96, 97, 101, 104, 145, 167, 175

six-cylinder 8, 16, 17, 18, 21, 27, 29, 33, 38, 39, 43, 47, 48, 49, 72, 77, 147, 184
spoiler 32, 43, 46, 50, 53, 56, 64, 65, 76, 96, 99, 100, 104, 106, 109, 114, 115, 116, 117, 126, 128, 133, 137, 139, 143, 144, 145, 152, 155, 159, 161, 170, 175, 179
Sports Car Club of America (SCCA) 52, 67, 90
SportsRoof 45, 46, 47, 49, 53, 56, 62, 65, 69, 71, 72, 76, 78, 79, 83, 104, 243, 244
Sprint 200 29
steering wheel 20, 21, 28, 34, 38, 47, 51, 56, 62, 63, 65, 72, 74, 91, 93, 94, 101, 110, 126, 139, 154, 161, 173, 176, 182
stroke 18, 39, 48, 63, 73, 98, 158, 160
subcompact 112
Sunshine Special 44
suspension 17, 19, 39, 40, 46, 50, 52, 53, 56, 57, 58, 63, 68, 74, 75, 76, 78, 80, 85, 90, 93, 94, 99, 102, 108, 113, 125, 126, 132, 134, 138, 139, 145, 146, 152, 157, 158, 159, 167, 169, 179, 182, 185, 192, 195, 196, 208, 210, 225, 231
SVO 121, 130, 131, 132, 133, 136, 137, 138, 139, 146, 147, 250, 251
SVT 67, 101, 108, 109, 145, 146, 153, 155, 156, 157, 159, 161, 162, 168, 169, 170, 172, 174, 175, 176, 257, 258, 259, 260, 261
sway bar 58, 117, 154, 157, 158, 159, 160

T-5 Mustang 30
tachometer 20, 47, 56, 66, 91, 98, 110, 114, 132
three-speed 16, 19, 21, 27, 33, 47, 72, 94, 98
traction bars 90, 94, 128, 129, 132
Trans-Am 52, 55, 67
transmission 12, 16, 19, 22, 27, 33, 41, 47, 48, 49, 54, 56, 64, 72, 74, 76, 78, 90, 94, 95, 108, 110, 113, 114, 115, 117, 127, 129, 130, 133, 134, 135, 152, 154, 155, 157, 158, 160, 161, 167, 168, 170, 173, 174, 175, 179, 193, 194, 205, 206, 210, 212, 231, 238, 239